VOLUME 6
DAVID SMALL TO GENE ZION

FAVORITE CHILDREN'S
AUTHORS AND
ILLUSTRATORS

E. RUSSELL PRIMM III, EDITOR IN CHIEF

TRADITION BOOKS™
EXCELSIOR, MINNESOTA

*For Irene Barron Keller, whose love of the English language touched
the lives of millions of young readers through her writing and editing*

❧

Published by **TRADITION BOOKS**™ and distributed to
the school and library market by **THE CHILD'S WORLD**®
P.O. Box 326, Chanhassen, MN 55317-0326
800/599-READ
http://www.childsworld.com

A NOTE TO OUR READERS:

The publication dates listed in each author or illustrator's selected bibliography represent the date of first publication in the United States.

The editors have listed literary awards that were announced prior to August 2002.

Every effort has been made to contact copyright holders of material included in this reference work. If any errors or omissions have occurred, corrections will be made in future editions.

Photographs ©: Albert Whitman and Company: 96; AP/Wide World Photos: 72, 116 (Harper-Collins); Candlewick Press: 92; Donald Sobol: 20; Harcourt: 24, 52, 124, 136; HarperCollins Publishers: 16 (Meredith Heuer), 40, 44, 48 (James Rapiequet Aclsmidt), 112, 132 (Joanne Ryder), 148; Houghton Mifflin Company: 76, 88 (Kurt Bomz), 108 (Peggy Morsch), 120; Kerlan Collection, University of Minnesota: 28 (Houghton Mifflin Company), 144 (Karen Hoyle); Penguin Putnam: 8, 12, 100, 140; Peter Spier: 32; Scholastic: 36, 56, 84, 128.

An Editorial Directions book

LIBRARY OF CONGRESS CATALOGING-IN-PUBLICATION DATA

Favorite children's authors and illustrators / E. Russell Primm, III, editor-in-chief.
    p. cm.
Summary: Provides biographical information about authors and illustrators of books for children and young adults, arranged in dictionary form. Includes bibliographical references and index.
  ISBN 1-59187-018-6 (v. 1 : lib. bdg. : alk. paper)—ISBN 1-59187-019-4 (v. 2 : lib. bdg. : alk. paper)—ISBN 1-59187-020-8 (v. 3 : lib. bdg. : alk. paper)—ISBN 1-59187-021-6 (v. 4 : lib. bdg. : alk. paper)—ISBN 1-59187-022-4 (v. 5 : lib. bdg. : alk. paper)—ISBN 1-59187-023-2 (v. 6 : lib. bdg. : alk. paper) 1. Children's literature—Bio-bibliography—Dictionaries—Juvenile literature. 2. Illustrators—Biography—Dictionaries—Juvenile literature. [1. Authors. 2. Illustrators.] I. Primm, E. Russell, 1958–
 PN1009.A1 F38 2002
 809'.89282'03—dc21   2002007129

TABLE OF CONTENTS

Major Children's Author and Illustrator Literary Awards

The American Book Award
Awarded from 1980 to 1983 in place of the National Book Award to give national recognition to achievement in several categories of children's literature

The Boston Globe-Horn Book Awards
Established in 1967 by Horn Book *magazine and the* Boston Globe *newspaper to honor the year's best fiction, poetry, nonfiction, and picture books for children*

The Caldecott Medal
Established in 1938 and presented by the Association for Library Service to Children division of the American Library Association to illustrators for the most distinguished picture book for children from the preceding year

The Carnegie Medal
Established in 1936 and presented by the British Library Association for an outstanding book for children written in English

The Carter G. Woodson Book Award
Established in 1974 and presented by the National Council for the Social Studies for the most distinguished social science books appropriate for young readers that depict ethnicity in the United States

The Coretta Scott King Awards
Established in 1970 in connection with the American Library Association to honor African-American authors and illustrators whose books are deemed outstanding, educational, and inspirational

The Hans Christian Andersen Medal
Established in 1956 by the International Board on Books for Young People to honor an author or illustrator, living at the time of nomination, whose complete works have made a lasting contribution to children's literature

THE KATE GREENAWAY MEDAL

Established by the Youth Libraries Group of the British Library Association in 1956 to honor illustrators of children's books published in the United Kingdom

THE LAURA INGALLS WILDER AWARD

Established by the Association for Library Service to Children division of the American Library Association in 1954 to honor an author or illustrator whose books, published in the United States, have made a substantial and lasting contribution to children's literature

THE MICHAEL L. PRINTZ AWARD

Established by the Young Adult Library Services division of the American Library Association in 2000 to honor literary excellence in young adult literature (fiction, nonfiction, poetry, or anthology)

THE NATIONAL BOOK AWARD

Established in 1950 to give national recognition to achievement in fiction, nonfiction, poetry, and young people's literature

THE NEWBERY MEDAL

Established in 1922 and presented by the Association for Library Service to Children division of the American Library Association for the most distinguished contribution to children's literature in the preceding year

THE ORBIS PICTUS AWARD FOR OUTSTANDING NONFICTION

Established in 1990 by the National Council of Teachers of English to honor an outstanding informational book published in the preceding year

THE PURA BELPRÉ AWARDS

Established in 1996 and cosponsored by the Association for Library Service to Children division of the American Library Association and the National Association to Promote Library Services to the Spanish Speaking to recognize a writer and illustrator of Latino or Latina background whose works affirm and celebrate the Latino experience

THE SCOTT O'DELL AWARD

Established in 1982 and presented by the O'Dell Award Committee to an American author who writes an outstanding tale of historical fiction for children or young adults that takes place in the New World

David Small

Born: February 12, 1945

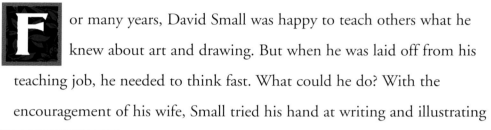

For many years, David Small was happy to teach others what he knew about art and drawing. But when he was laid off from his teaching job, he needed to think fast. What could he do? With the encouragement of his wife, Small tried his hand at writing and illustrating books for children.

Since his first book was published in 1982, David Small has created nearly thirty books for kids. He has earned fans far and wide for his fun stories and bright, colorful pictures.

David Small was born on February 12, 1945, in Detroit, Michigan. As a boy, he was very sick. David spent a lot of time in bed trying to get better. During that time, he often read books or drew pictures. David's mother recognized his special talent and signed him up for Saturday art classes at the Detroit Institute of Arts. Although David hated the

------

AS A BOY, DAVID SMALL SPENT MANY SUMMERS ON HIS GRANDPARENTS' FARM IN INDIANA. THERE, HE LEARNED TO LOVE ANIMALS AND THE COUNTRY.

classes, he loved looking through the museum. He enjoyed roaming the big building, examining the pictures, armor, and other items.

When Small entered Wayne State Univeristy, his interest in art really blossomed. He spent as much time as he could working on his art. He knew he wanted to focus on art and drawing when he graduated. After earning a master of fine arts degree from Yale University in 1972, Small began teaching art to college students. In time, he turned to illustrating—and writing—children's books.

"Though I always dreamed of being an artist, it was not until I was in my late thirties and had several works published that I began to say, proudly, 'I am an artist.' I took it that seriously."

Small's stories usually carry a positive message. Many of his books focus on independent characters who are different from others. One of Small's most popular books is *Imogene's Antlers*. The story about a girl who sprouts antlers overnight is a favorite of kids everywhere. The book has sold more than a million copies and been translated into many different languages.

It usually takes Small about a year to create a book from start to finish. Although he prefers writing and illustrating his own ideas, Small also enjoys drawing pictures for the stories of other authors. Over the years, he has brought to life the works of several famous writers. They

---

SOME OF SMALL'S BOOK ILLUSTRATIONS HANG ON THE WALL OF HIS OFFICE.
HE CALLS THE PICTURES HIS "FAMILY PORTRAITS."

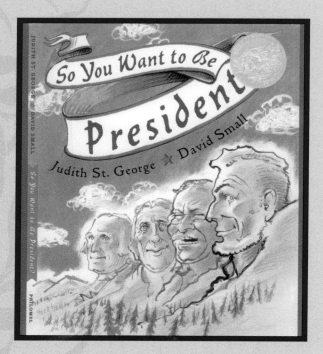

A Selected Bibliography of Small's Work

So You Want to Be an Inventor? (2002)
The Journey (Illustrations only, 2001)
So You Want to Be President? (Illustrations only, 2000)
The Library (Illustrations only, 1999)
The Gardener (Illustrations only, 1997)
Hoover's Bride (1995)
George Washington's Cows (1994)
The Money Tree (Illustrations only, 1994)
Box and Cox (Illustrations only, 1990)
As: A Surfeit of Similes (Illustrations only, 1989)
Imogene's Antlers (1985)
Eulalie and the Hopping Head (1982)

Small's Major Literary Awards

2001 Caldecott Medal
  So You Want to Be President?

1998 Caldecott Honor Book
  The Gardener

include Carl Sandburg, Jonathan Swift, Beverly Cleary, Russell Hoban, and Norton Juster. He also worked with author Judith St. George on *So You Want to Be President?*, which won the Caldecott Medal in 2001.

One of Small's favorite writers to work with is Sarah Stewart. Stewart is not only a talented children's author— she's Small's wife! Together, the couple has created several popular books for children, including *The Library, The Gardener,* and *The Journey. The Gardener* was named a Caldecott Honor Book.

"I'm a perfectionist, but it's good to set high standards for yourself."

Small and Stewart live in a big, old house in Mendon, Michigan. Small has livened up their home by painting pictures of insects, plants, and other things all over the walls.

In addition to children's books, David Small draws editorial cartoons for such papers as the *New York Times,* the *Wall Street Journal,* and the *Washington Post.* His pictures also appear in national magazines. Fans of Small's children's books can rest assured that they'll see more of his illustrations in the future. This talented artist believes that his best work is yet to come.

❧

WHERE TO FIND OUT MORE ABOUT DAVID SMALL

BOOKS
Holtze, Sally Holmes, ed.
Sixth Book of Junior Authors & Illustrators.
New York: H. W. Wilson Company, 1989.

WEB SITES
NATIONAL CENTER FOR CHILDREN'S
ILLUSTRATED LITERATURE
http://www.nccil.org/exhibit/davidsmall.html
For a biography of David Small

PARENTS' CHOICE
http://www.parents-choice.org/full_abstract.cfm?art_id=22&the_page=editorials
To learn more about Small's life

SMALL'S FIRST BOOK, PUBLISHED IN 1982, WAS *EULALIE AND THE HOPPING HEAD.* SMALL SENT THE BOOK TO MORE THAN TWENTY PUBLISHERS BEFORE IT WAS FINALLY ACCEPTED.

Lane Smith

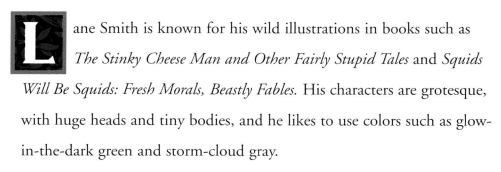

Born: August 25, 1959

Lane Smith is known for his wild illustrations in books such as *The Stinky Cheese Man and Other Fairly Stupid Tales* and *Squids Will Be Squids: Fresh Morals, Beastly Fables.* His characters are grotesque, with huge heads and tiny bodies, and he likes to use colors such as glow-in-the-dark green and storm-cloud gray.

Some people find his pictures dark and disturbing. "When I was a child, I *liked* dark things," Smith explains. He loved monster movies and Halloween and the scratching of branches against the windows on rainy nights.

Smith was born on August 25, 1959, in Oklahoma, but he grew up in California with his parents and his brother Shane. ("Shane and Lane. My mom thought that was funny," Smith says. "Yeah, a real hoot.") Smith attended California Art Center College of Design in Pasadena. He studied advertising art, but

LANE SMITH WAS CHOSEN TO DO NEW ILLUSTRATIONS FOR ONE OF THE BOOKS DR. SEUSS LEFT UNFINISHED AT THE TIME OF HIS DEATH. *HOORAY FOR DIFFENDOOFER DAY!* ALSO CONTAINED NEW MATERIAL WRITTEN BY JACK PRELUTSKY.

he became interested in pop art and European illustration. His teachers told him he would never find a job.

Smith was lucky, though. He moved to New York and discovered that many magazine editors wanted "punk" and "new wave" illustration—just the kind of thing that he liked to draw. He was soon working for magazines such as *Rolling Stone, Ms.,* and *Time.*

His first children's book was a Halloween-themed alphabet book. Lane painted pictures for all the letters of the alphabet. Then an author named Eve Merriam took the pictures and wrote poems to fit them. *Halloween ABC* was published in 1987.

A Selected Bibliography of Smith's Work

Pinocchio, the Boy: Incognito in Collodi (2002)

Baloney, Henry P. (Illustrations only, 2001)

The Very Persistent Gappers of Frip (Illustrations only, 2000)

It's All Greek to Me (Illustrations only, 1999)

Hooray for Diffendoofer Day! (Illustrations only, 1998)

Squids Will Be Squids: Fresh Morals, Beastly Fables (1998)

James and the Giant Peach (Illustrations only, 1996)

Tut, Tut (Illustrations only, 1996)

Math Curse (Illustrations only, 1995)

The Happy Hocky Family (1993)

The Stinky Cheese Man and Other Fairly Stupid Tales (Illustrations only, 1992)

The Big Pets (1991)

Glasses: Who Needs 'Em? (1991)

Time Warp Trio: Knights of the Kitchen Table (Illustrations only, 1991)

Time Warp Trio: The Not-So-Jolly Roger (Illustrations only, 1991)

Flying Jake (1989)

The True Story of the 3 Little Pigs! (Illustrations only, 1989)

Halloween ABC (Illustrations only, 1987)

Smith's Major Literary Awards

1993 Caldecott Honor Book
   The Stinky Cheese Man and Other Fairly Stupid Tales

Smith has created several books on his own, including *Flying Jake* and *Glasses: Who Needs 'Em?*. But his best-known work has been with Jon Scieszka, a teacher and aspiring writer he met in the 1980s. Scieszka's sense of humor fits well with Smith's drawing style. The first book the two did together was *The True Story of the 3 Little Pigs!*, published in 1989, in which the wolf, the villain of the tale, explains why he is innocent. It took a long time to find a publisher for the strange book. But once the book was published, it became wildly popular—even the writer and artist were surprised.

Smith and Sciezska were invited to speak at schools. They started telling other twisted-around versions of fairy tales to entertain the children they met. These tales became *The Stinky Cheese Man and Other Fairly Stupid Tales,* another very popular book. In *The Stinky Cheese Man,* the ugly duckling grows up to be an ugly duck, and a princess kisses a frog only to discover that he's just kidding about being a prince. The book has

> *"Most of the magazine work I do, they'll call Monday and need it finished by Wednesday. If I really buckle down, I can probably do a painting a day, but I like to take a lot of breaks."*

> *"I just love the print medium. I always thought it would be kind of depressing to work for months on a painting and then . . . have it hang in somebody's house."*

To earn money for college, Smith worked as a janitor at Disneyland. He spent the nights cleaning out the Haunted Mansion and rides such as the Revolving Teacups.

many jokes about bookmaking, too. The title page is in the wrong spot, the dedication is upside-down, and several characters are crushed when the table of contents falls onto the page.

Scieszka and Smith have created several other picture books together. They also started the Time Warp Trio series, about three boys who travel through time and have goofy adventures.

A reporter once asked Lane Smith whether he planned to keep on doing silly work "There are so many serious books out there and lots of people who do them really well," Smith told him. "But there aren't many people who do really goofy work."

❧

WHERE TO FIND OUT MORE ABOUT LANE SMITH

BOOKS

Kovacs, Deborah, and James Preller. *Meet the Authors and Illustrators: 60 Creators of Favorite Children's Books Talk about Their Work.* Vol. 2. New York: Scholastic, 1993.

WEB SITES

KIDSREAD.COM
http://www.kidsreads.com/series/series-warp-author.asp#lane
For information about Jon Scieszka and Lane Smith

TIME FOR KIDS
http://www.timeforkids.com/TFK/magazines/story/0,6277,88538,00.html
For an interview with Lane Smith and Jon Scieszka

———

LANE'S FIRST MEETING WITH SCIEZSKA WASN'T VERY SUCCESSFUL. THE TWO WENT TO THE BRONX ZOO IN NEW YORK. SMITH WANTED TO TALK, BUT SCIEZSKA JUST TOLD KNOCK-KNOCK JOKES. "I THOUGHT, WHAT'S WITH THIS GUY?" SMITH REMEMBERS.

Lemony Snicket

Born: 1970

Lemony Snicket didn't like many of the books that he read as a child. He thought they were too happy, and he didn't like happy endings—or happy beginnings or happy middles. And so the unlikely children's author wrote about all the things that parents want to shield their children from. He wrote about the disasters that descend on the unluckiest of children. He wrote about parents killed by fire, orphans hated by their relatives, and children forever on the run from a cruel villain. He wrote, in short, A Series of Unfortunate Events, and along the way, he made legions of children very happy.

Lemony Snicket likes to say that his own childhood was unspeak-

---

DANIEL HANDLER FIRST USED THE NAME LEMONY SNICKET WHEN HE WAS RESEARCHING A BOOK. HE DIDN'T WANT THE PEOPLE HE WAS WRITING ABOUT TO KNOW WHO HE WAS.

ably dreadful, but Lemony Snicket is, in fact, not a real person at all. He is the creation of Daniel Handler, whose own childhood seems not to have been so bad. He was born in 1970 in San Francisco, California. Unlike the unfortunate children in his books, his parents were not killed by fire. One is an accountant, and one a college dean. Handler went to school at San Francisco's Lowell High School, received a good education, and graduated with an award for the best personality. That doesn't sound so bad. Handler then went to Wesleyan University in Middletown, Connecticut. He started to write poetry and in 1990

> *"There are species of insects which spend their entire lives in filthy underground caverns. Compared to those species of insects—and certain others—my childhood was 'happy' indeed."*
> *—Lemony Snicket*

won a prize from the Academy of American Poets. His love of poets can be seen in the names of the characters in his books: the Beaudelaire children are named after a famous French poet. There is also a Mr. Poe, named for Edgar Allan Poe, the American poet who himself wrote rather morbid tales.

After graduating from college, Handler received an Olin Fellowship to write a novel. He also worked as a comedy writer for a radio program called "The House of Blues Radio Hour." It might seem odd that the

THE AUDIO VERSION OF LEMONY SNICKET'S *THE BAD BEGINNING* WAS NOMINATED FOR A GRAMMY AWARD FOR THE BEST SPOKEN WORD ALBUM FOR CHILDREN.

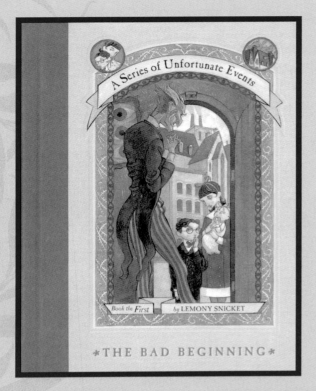

THE BAD BEGINNING

A Selected Bibliography of Snicket's Work

Lemony Snicket: the Unauthorized Autobiography. (2002)

The Ersatz Elevator (2001)

The Hostile Hospital (2001)

The Vile Village (2001)

The Austere Academy (2000)

The Miserable Mill (2000)

The Wide Window (2000)

The Bad Beginning (1999)

The Reptile Room (1999)

morbid Mr. Handler was a comedy writer, but beneath his dreary statements is a wry smile. His two adult novels both deal with the dark humor of bad situations. When an editor suggested he turn his wicked humor into children's books, his book series called A Series of Unfortunate Events was the outcome.

Under the name Lemony Snicket, Handler writes about the misadventures of the three Beaudelaire children: Violet, Klaus, and Sunny. The children are clever and speak in a deadpan manner. Handler believes that kids are smart, and his writing is complicated and witty. Snicket himself often butts into the story to make a few remarks about the writing style and to warn readers of especially dreadful things to come.

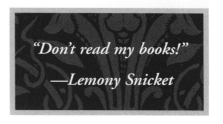

"Don't read my books!"
—*Lemony Snicket*

Lemony Snicket also warns his readers not to read his books. But no one is listening—his books are frequently on best-seller lists. They have delighted children who find dreadful things funny and who like the strange Lemony Snicket, even if Daniel Handler sometimes pretends that he doesn't exist.

WHERE TO FIND OUT MORE ABOUT LEMONY SNICKET

BOOKS

Snicket, Lemony. *Lemony Snicket: The Unauthorized Autobiography.* New York: HarperCollins, 2002.

WEB SITES

DYMOCKS BOOKSELLERS
http://www.dymocks.com.au/asp/lemonysnicket.asp
For the transcript of an interview with Snicket

HARPERCHILDRENS.COM
http://www.harperchildrens.com/hch/author/author/snicket/
For information about a poetry contest and some frequently asked questions about Lemony Sincket's secretive life

LEMONY SNICKET
www.lemonysnicket.com/
For as much autobiographical information as Lemony Snicket is willing to offer, a booklist, and some frequently asked questions

WHEN HANDLER SHOWS UP AT BOOK READINGS, HE EXPLAINS THAT HE IS STANDING IN FOR LEMONY SNICKET. HE LIKES TO MAKE UP FOR SNICKET'S ABSENCE BY PLAYING THE ACCORDION.

Donald Sobol

Born: October 4, 1924

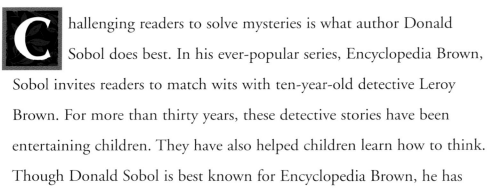

Challenging readers to solve mysteries is what author Donald Sobol does best. In his ever-popular series, Encyclopedia Brown, Sobol invites readers to match wits with ten-year-old detective Leroy Brown. For more than thirty years, these detective stories have been entertaining children. They have also helped children learn how to think. Though Donald Sobol is best known for Encyclopedia Brown, he has written historical novels and biographies of famous people as well.

Donald Sobol was born in New York City on October 4, 1924, to Ira J. and Ida Sobol. As a youngster, he dreamed of becoming a singer, a sculptor, and a baseball player, but he soon found these goals quite unreachable. After graduating from the Fieldston School in New York City, Sobol enlisted in the U.S. Army Corp of Engi-

TWENTY-SIX PUBLISHERS REJECTED DONALD SOBOL'S FIRST BOOK IN THE ENCYCLOPEDIA BROWN SERIES BEFORE THE T. NELSON PUBLISHING COMPANY FINALLY PUBLISHED IT IN 1963.

neers and served three years in World War II (1939–1945).

After leaving the army in 1946, he enrolled at Oberlin College in Ohio, where he graduated with a bachelor's degree in English. While Sobol was at Oberlin, an English professor helped him develop his talent for writing.

For the next eight years, Sobol wrote under different names for magazines. Because the pay was low, he had to take

> *"Stories originate in two ways. They start from a writer's own experience, or they start from his imagination. Most of my stories depend upon my imagination."*

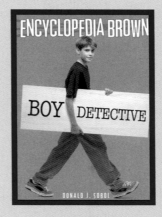

A Selected Bibliography of Sobol's Work

Encyclopedia Brown and the Case of the Slippery Salamander (1999)

Encyclopedia Brown and the Case of the Sleeping Dog (1998)

Encyclopedia Brown and the Case of the Disgusting Sneakers (1990)

Encyclopedia Brown and the Case of the Treasure Hunt (1988)

Encyclopedia Brown's Book of Wacky Cars (1987)

Encyclopedia Brown's Third Record Book of Weird and Wonderful Facts (1985)

Encyclopedia Brown's Book of Wacky Animals (1985)

Encyclopedia Brown's Book of Wacky Spies (1984)

Encyclopedia Brown Takes the Cake!: A Cook and Case Book (1983)

Encyclopedia Brown Sets the Pace (1982)

Angie's First Case (1981)

Encyclopedia Brown's Second Record Book of Weird and Wonderful Facts (1981)

Encyclopedia Brown Carries On (1980)

Encyclopedia Brown and the Case of the Midnight Visitor (1977)

Encyclopedia Brown and the Case of the Dead Eagles (1976)

Encyclopedia Brown Lends a Hand (1974)

Encyclopedia Brown Takes the Case: Ten All-New Mysteries (1973)

Greta the Strong (1970)

Encyclopedia Brown Keeps the Peace (1969)

Encyclopedia Brown Solves Them All (1968)

Encyclopedia Brown Gets His Man (1967)

Secret Agents Four (1967)

Encyclopedia Brown Finds the Clues (1966)

Encyclopedia Brown and the Case of the Secret Pitch: Ten All-New Mysteries (1965)

Encyclopedia Brown, Boy Detective (1963)

The First Book of Medieval Man (1959)

The Lost Dispatch: A Story of Antietam (1958)

The Double Quest (1957)

extra jobs to support himself. From 1946 to 1952, he worked as a
reporter with the *New York Sun* and the *Long Island Daily Press.* Then he
worked briefly as a buyer for R. H. Macy in New York City. In 1954, at
the age of thirty, Sobol made a daring move. He quit his jobs to write
full-time.

A year later, he married
Rose Tiplitz, an engineer.
Together, they had four children.
In 1961, they moved to Florida
for the winter. They have lived
there ever since.

Donald Sobol published
his first book in 1957. Called *The Double Quest,* it is a mystery about
knights in medieval times. *The Double Quest* and Sobol's next two
books—*The Lost Dispatch: A Story of Antietam,* published in 1958, and
The First Book of Medieval Man, published in 1959—are young adult
books. They were well received but never became as popular as the
Encyclopedia Brown books that Sobol began to publish in 1963.

The first title of the series, *Encyclopedia Brown, Boy Detective,* set
the pattern for the more than twenty books that followed. Each book
contains ten short mysteries on pages filled with jokes. Readers need to

> *"[The advice] 'Write about what you know' had limited me to my own experiences and so forced me to rely solely upon my imagination. 'Know what you write about' set me free. . . . [I] went to the library and dug up all the information I could find."*

THE ENCYCLOPEDIA BROWN SERIES HAS BEEN TRANSLATED INTO THIRTEEN LANGUAGES AND BRAILLE. SOME OF THEM HAVE BEEN MADE INTO COMIC STRIPS. IN 1989, *ENCYCLOPEDIA BROWN, BOY DETECTIVE* WAS MADE INTO A MOVIE FOR HBO TELEVISION.

do good detective work to discover the clues in the stories and solve the cases without reading the solutions in the back of the book.

Many people compare Donald Sobol's popular Encyclopedia Brown series to the Hardy Boys and Nancy Drew mysteries of the past. For generations, these series have been outwitting readers and making them laugh. Donald Sobol's books will continue to do that for decades to come.

و

WHERE TO FIND OUT MORE ABOUT DONALD SOBOL

BOOKS

Chevalier, Tracy, ed. *Twentieth-Century Children's Writers.* Chicago: St. James Press, 1989.

De Montreville, Doris, and Elizabeth D. Crawford, eds. *Fourth Book of Junior Authors & Illustrators.* New York: H. W. Wilson Company, 1978.

WEB SITES

HALL KIDS TALES
http://hallkidstales.com/S/22.shtml
For links to reviews and synopses of Sobol's books

KIDSREAD.COM
http://www.kidsreads.com/series/series-brown-author.asp
For information about Sobol's life and work

———

WHEN ASKED IF ENCYCLOPEDIA BROWN IS A REAL BOY, DONALD SOBOL SAYS, "HE IS, PERHAPS, THE BOY I WANTED TO BE—DOING THE THINGS I WANTED TO READ ABOUT BUT COULD NOT FIND IN ANY BOOK WHEN I WAS TEN."

Gary Soto

Born: April 12, 1952

Growing up in a working-class Mexican-American neighborhood has had a strong influence on Gary Soto's writing. His books of poetry and short stories for children and young people include memories of his Mexican-American heritage. Some of Soto's best-known books for young people are *Baseball in April and Other Stories, A Fire in My Hands: A Book of Poems, Taking Sides,* and *Neighborhood Odes.*

Soto was born on April 12, 1952, in Fresno, California. Soto's grandparents had come to the United States from Mexico in the 1930s. Soto's parents were born in the United States, but remembered their heritage.

GARY SOTO IS ONE OF THE YOUNGEST POETS TO HAVE HIS WORK PUBLISHED IN *THE NORTON ANTHOLOGY OF MODERN POETRY.*

Gary Soto's parents worked in the fields picking grapes, oranges, and cotton. His father got a job in a factory that packed raisins. When Gary was about five years old, his father died in an accident at the factory. His mother had to raise her three children alone.

Gary's family was poor, and his mother worked hard to provide for her children. Gary did not have books as a child and was not encouraged to read. "I don't think I had any literary aspirations when I was a kid," Soto remembers. "So my wanting to write poetry was sort of a fluke." He did not become interested in writing and poetry until he entered college.

> *"One of the things I would like to do is make that leap from being a Chicano writer to being simply a writer."*

In 1970, Soto graduated from high school and enrolled at Fresno City College. He planned to study geography, but after taking a poetry class, he became interested in creative writing. Soto loved the poetry that he read for class, and he learned a great deal about poetry from his professors. Soto graduated from college in 1974 and went on to get a master's degree in creative writing.

In 1977, Soto was hired to teach at the University of California at Irvine. He worked as a professor of Chicano studies and English. That same year, he published his first book of poetry for adults, *The Elements*

SOTO WROTE THE LYRICS FOR THE OPERA *NERDLANDIA,* WHICH
WAS PERFORMED BY THE LOS ANGELES OPERA.

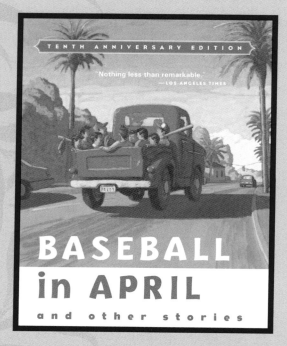

A Selected Bibliography of Soto's Work

If the Shoe Fits (2002)
Poetry Lover (2001)
Nickel and Dime (2000)
A Natural Man (1999)
Big Bushy Mustache (1998)
Buried Onions (1997)
Boys at Work (1995)
Canto Familiar (1995)
Chato's Kitchen (1995)
Summer on Wheels (1995)
Too Many Tamales (1993)
A Fire in My Hands: A Book of Poems (1992)
Neighborhood Odes (1992)
Pacific Crossing (1992)
The Skirt (1992)
Taking Sides (1991)
Baseball in April and Other Stories (1990)
A Summer Life (1990)

Soto's Major Literary Awards

1996 Pura Belpré Honor Book for Narrative
Baseball in April and Other Stories

of San Joaquin. In 1985, he won an American Book Award for the memoir *Living up the Street: Narrative Recollections.* Soto did not complete his first book specifically for young people until 1990 when *Baseball in April and Other Stories* was published.

In his stories and poetry, Gary Soto writes about life in his Mexican-American neighborhood. He writes about what life was like in large cities and tells stories about the hard work that Mexican Americans did in the fields. In his stories for young people, he writes about realistic situations and conflicts. Most young people can identify with the characters in Soto's books.

In addition to being a

writer, Soto has taught creative writing at colleges and universities. He lives in Berkeley, California, with his wife and daughter. He continues to write poetry, stories, and plays for young people and adults.

"To me the finest praise is when a reader says, 'I can see your stories.' This is what I'm always working for, a story that becomes alive and meaningful in the reader's mind."

WHERE TO FIND OUT MORE ABOUT GARY SOTO

BOOKS

Drew, Bernard A. *The 100 Most Popular Young Adult Authors: Biographical Sketches and Bibliographies.* Englewood, Colo.: Libraries Unlimited, 1997.

Hill, Christine M. *Ten Terrific Authors for Teens.* Berkeley Heights, N.J.: Enslow, 2000.

Machamer, Gene. *The Illustrated Hispanic American Profiles.* Mechanicsburg, Pa.: Carlisle Press, 1993.

Soto, Gary. *A Summer Life.* Hanover, N.H.: University Press of New England, 1990.

WEB SITES

EDUCATIONAL PAPERBACK ASSOCIATION
http://www.edupaperback.org/authorbios/Soto_Gary.html
For a biography of Soto and other information

THE OFFICIAL GARY SOTO WEB SITE
http://www.garysoto.com/
For information about Gary Soto's life and work

WHEN GARY SOTO WAS YOUNG, HE WANTED TO BE A PRIEST OR A PALEONTOLOGIST, A SCIENTIST WHO STUDIES FOSSILS AND DINOSAUR BONES.

Elizabeth George Speare

Born: November 21, 1908
Died: November 15, 1994

I f you have ever thought that early American history was a little on the dry side, Elizabeth George Speare might change your mind. Her books capture the struggle of early Americans while telling a rip-roaring story. She wrote about settlers being captured by Native Americans and told stories about life in the colonies. One of her tales is about an orphaned girl sailing from Barbados to live with a relative in Connecticut. She becomes friends with a woman who is believed to be a witch—at a time when being a witch could bring the whole village carrying torches and calling for blood.

Elizabeth George Speare started writing at a young age. She was born in Melrose, Massachusetts, on November 21, 1908, the daughter of an architect, Harry Allan George, and his wife, Demetria. Elizabeth grew up in a typical New England setting. She

---

ELIZABETH GEORGE SPEARE RECEIVED THE NEWBERY MEDAL TWICE, IN 1959 FOR *THE WITCH OF BLACKBIRD POND* AND IN 1962 FOR *THE BRONZE BOW.*

took walks in the woods, picked blueberries, and traveled to the seaside during the summer. She could often be found reading and dreaming. She loved stories and began to write her own to pass the days.

Speare attended Boston University, where she earned a bachelor's degree and a master's degree. After she graduated, she wanted to share her love of stories with children, so she taught English in high schools.

> *"I began to write from the age of eight on. I filled volumes of brown note-books with poetry and stories, all more incredibly naive than any child could write today."*

Elizabeth George Speare

The WITCH of Blackbird Pond

A Selected Bibliography of Speare's Work

The Sign of the Beaver (1983)
Ice Glen (1967)
The Prospering (1967)
Life in Colonial America (1963)
The Bronze Bow (1961)
The Witch of Blackbird Pond (1958)
Calico Captive (1957)

Speare's Major Literary Awards

1989 Laura Ingalls Wilder Award

1984 Newbery Honor Book
1984 Scott O'Dell Award
   The Sign of the Beaver

1962 Newbery Medal
   The Bronze Bow

1959 Newbery Medal
   The Witch of Blackbird Pond

In 1936, she married Alden Speare, an industrial engineer, and moved to Wethersfield, Connecticut. The couple had two children, Alden Jr. and Mary Elizabeth. While her children were young, Speare spent time at home. But she never lost her interest in stories.

Moving to Connecticut prompted Speare to start reading about the region. She began to write about Connecticut and its history. Her articles were published in various magazines, and one was adapted for television.

During her research, Speare discovered a diary from 1796 of a young woman who had been held captive by Native Americans. The 200-year-old book, *The Narrative of the Captivity of Mrs. Johnson,* prompted Speare to retell the story for young readers. The result, *Calico Captive,* brought out the personalities of two sisters captured by Native Americans after an evening party, while remaining true to the setting of the actual story. The book was praised for presenting historical fiction with a real pulse.

"[During the writing of the The Witch of Blackbird Pond,*] Kit Tyler and her imaginary family and friends came to seem very real to me, and when this book won the Newbery Medal in 1959, I was happy to know they had made so many friends for themselves."*

Speare chose her own town of Wethersfield as the setting for her next book, *The Witch of Blackbird Pond.* The characters were her own creation, but the

SPEARE LOVED THE HISTORICAL RESEARCH THAT ALLOWED HER TO WRITE HER HISTORICAL FICTION. SHE SAID THAT SHE COULD SPEND HOURS AND HOURS RESEARCHING ONE MINOR DETAIL OF A BOOK.

setting is New England in 1687, and Speare ferreted out all the records she could from the period and consulted local historians.

Speare's interest in early American history also led to her writing *Life in Colonial America,* a nonfiction book. But Elizabeth George Speare is best remembered for her ability to breathe life into history through the telling of gripping stories. She died on November 15, 1994.

❧

WHERE TO FIND OUT MORE ABOUT ELIZABETH GEORGE SPEARE

BOOKS

Apseloff, Marilyn Fain. *Elizabeth George Speare.* New York: Twayne Publications, 1992.

Kovacs, Deborah, and James Preller. *Meet the Authors and Illustrators: 60 Creators of Favorite Children's Books Talk about Their Work.* Vol.1. New York: Scholastic, 1993.

McElmeel, Sharron L. *100 Most Popular Children's Authors: Biographical Sketches and Bibliographies.* Englewood, Colo.: Libraries Unlimited, 1999.

WEB SITES

CAROL HURST'S CHILDREN'S LITERATURE SITE
http://www.carolhurst.com/titles/signofthe.html
To read a review of *The Sign of the Beaver*

EDUCATIONAL PAPERBACK ASSOCIATION
http://www.edupaperback.org/authorbios/Speare_ElizabethGeorge.html
For more information about Speare's life and work

RANDOM HOUSE
http://www.randomhouse.com/teachers/authors/spea.html
For a brief biography of Speare

――――

DURING THE LAST YEARS OF HER LIFE, SPEARE WORKED WITH RESEARCHERS AT THE UNIVERSITY OF CONNECTICUT TO HELP SIMPLIFY THE LIVES OF HANDICAPPED HOMEMAKERS.

Peter Spier

Born: June 6, 1927

Peter Spier has illustrated more than forty books that he wrote. He has also illustrated more than 150 books for other authors. Along the way, he has won a Caldecott Medal, the highest honor a children's book illustrator can earn. Spier's books include *Noah's Ark, The Fox Went Out on a Chilly Night: An Old Song, People,* and *Bored—Nothing to Do!*

Peter Spier was born on June 6, 1927, in Amsterdam, the Netherlands. He grew up in a town called Broek-in-Waterland. Another famous person who grew up in this town was Hans Brinker, the young boy who supposedly rescued his village from flooding by sticking his finger in a dike.

SPIER'S BOOKS HAVE BEEN TRANSLATED INTO TWENTY-FOUR LANGUAGES.

Peter and his brother and sister all went to school in the city of Amsterdam. They lived near the sea, and the family spent their weekends sailing. Peter enjoyed being on the water. As an adult, he still sails. He also builds model ships.

Peter's father was a journalist and political cartoonist. Peter watched his father work, and he began to draw, too. By the time he finished high school in 1945, he knew he wanted to be an artist, so he enrolled in a school to study art. Two years later, Spier had to serve in the Netherlands's navy. He traveled to the West Indies and South America.

Peter Spier left the navy in 1951 and got a job for the largest

"If you don't know what it looks like, don't draw it."

newspaper in the Netherlands. First he was assigned to work in Paris, France, and then in the United States. After working for awhile in Houston, Texas, Spier decided to move to New York and illustrate children's books.

The first book he illustrated was *Cocoa,* which was written by Margaret G. Otto. It was published in 1953. For the next eight years, Spier illustrated books for other authors. Then, in 1961, Spier illustrated a folk song in *The Fox Went Out on a Chilly Night: An Old Song.* It was instantly popular and was named a Caldecott Honor Book.

PETER SPIER BECAME A U.S. CITIZEN IN 1958.

NOAH'S ARK

Illustrated by **PETER SPIER**

A Selected Bibliography of Spier's Work

Father, May I Come? (1993)

The Book of Jonah (1985)

Trucks, Trucks, Trucks (Illustrations only, 1984)

Peter Spier's Rain (1982)

People (1980)

The Legend of New Amsterdam (1979)

Bored—Nothing to Do! (1978)

Noah's Ark (1977)

The Star-Spangled Banner (Illustrations only, 1973)

Tin Lizzie (1975)

The Erie Canal (1970)

London Bridge Is Falling Down! (1967)

To Market! To Market! (1967)

The Fox Went Out on a Chilly Night: An Old Song (1961)

The Cow Who Fell in the Canal (Illustrations only, 1957)

Cocoa (Illustrations only, 1953)

Spier's Major Literary Awards

1982 American Book Award

1978 Caldecott Medal
   Noah's Ark

1967 *Boston Globe–Horn Book* Picture Book Award
   London Bridge Is Falling Down!

1962 Caldecott Honor Book
   The Fox Went Out on a Chilly Night: An Old Song

Since then, many of Spier's books have won awards. He is known for his careful, detailed illustrations. In fact, some of his books have very few or no words. One of these books is *Noah's Ark,* which retells the well-known Bible story almost entirely in pictures. In his *Peter Spier's Rain,* Spier uses only pictures to tell the story of a brother and sister caught in a rainstorm.

"None of [the other retellings of the story] shows Noah shoveling manure or even hinted at the stench and the mess inside. It was then that I knew that there was room for one more Noah's Ark."

Children and adults enjoy Peter Spier's illustrations. They like the vitality and humor of his drawings. In the book entitled *People,* Spier drew fifty-four different noses on one page!

Spier continue to win awards, and some of his books have been made into videos. He lives with his wife in Shoreham, New York, where he continues to write and illustrate children's books. "As long as your hand is steady, you can keep on making books for as long as you wish. The wonderful thing for me is I don't *have* to do it anymore. I'm doing it because it's still fun." says Spier.

❧

WHERE TO FIND OUT MORE ABOUT PETER SPIER

BOOKS

De Montveville, Dorris, and Donna Hill, eds. *Third Book of Junior Authors.* New York: H. W. Wilson Company, 1972

Kovacs, Deborah, and James Preller. *Meet the Authors and Illustrators: 60 Creators of Favorite Children's Books Talk about Their Work.* Vol. 2. New York: Scholastic, 1993.

WEB SITES

HALL KIDS TALES
http://hallkidstales.com/S/25.shtml
For a list of Spier's books with links to summaries and reviews

MCCAIN LIBRARY AND ARCHIVES
http://www.lib.usm.edu/%7Edegrum/html/research/findaids/spier.htm
To find biographical information about Spier

SPIER CREATED THE MOTHER GOOSE LIBRARY SERIES IN 1967. HE SELECTED, ADAPTED, AND ILLUSTRATED EACH BOOK IN THE SERIES.

Jerry Spinelli

Born: February 1, 1941

When kids ask Jerry Spinelli where he gets his ideas for his books, his answer is simple: "I get them from you. You're the funny ones." His humorous books for young people have made Spinelli an award-winning author. His best-known books for young people include *Maniac Magee, Space Station Seventh Grade,* and *There's a Girl in My Hammerlock.*

Spinelli was born on February 1, 1941, in Norristown, Pennsylvania. He did not spend much time reading or writing when he was young. Instead, he spent most of his time playing baseball. Jerry played on Little League teams as well as in junior and senior high school. He dreamed of being a major league baseball player.

Jerry did not think of becoming a

SPINELLI'S FAVORITE BOOK OF HIS IS *MANIAC MAGEE.*
HE LIKES "THE MESSAGE, THE STORY, AND THE LANGUAGE."

writer until he was about sixteen years old. His high school's football team won a big game, and everyone was celebrating. Jerry had a different way to celebrate. He wrote a poem about the game, which was published in the local newspaper a few days later. Jerry quickly became interested in becoming a writer.

After graduating from high school, Jerry Spinelli attended

"Now I don't really write for adults or kids—I don't write for kids, I write about them. I think you need to do that, otherwise you end up preaching down. You need to listen not so much to the audience but to the story itself."

A Selected Bibliography of Spinelli's Work

Loser (2002)
Stargirl (2000)
Knots in My Yo-Yo String: The Autobiography of a Kid (1998)
Wringer (1997)
Crash (1996)
Do the Funky Pickle (1992)
Fourth Grade Rats (1991)
School Daze: Report to the Principal's Office (1991)
There's a Girl in My Hammerlock (1991)
Maniac Magee (1990)
The Bathwater Gang (1990)
Dump Days (1988)
Jason and Marceline (1986)
Night of the Whale (1985)
Who Put That Hair in My Toothbrush? (1984)
Space Station Seventh Grade (1982)

Spinelli's Major Literary Awards

1998 Newbery Honor Book
   Wringer
1991 Newbery Medal
1990 *Boston Globe–Horn Book* Fiction Award
   Maniac Magee

Gettysburg College and Johns Hopkins University. When he finished college, he took a job as an editor for a magazine. He also began writing novels for adults. Spinelli used his lunch breaks to write. He wrote four novels for adults but was not able to find anyone to publish them.

In 1977, Spinelli married Eileen Mesi, who is also a writer. Eileen already had six children, so Spinelli became an instant father.

Being the father to six children changed Spinelli's career as a writer. Spinelli found the inspiration for his first published book, *Space Station Seventh Grade,* by observing his own children. "For the first two books, I didn't even have to look outside my own house," Spinelli says.

> *"I like to let it be chaotic, so possibilities can reign and prevail. Out of that mess, gradually, hopefully, a story will begin to take shape."*

Spinelli also gets ideas for his books from his memories of growing up in a small town. "I thought I was simply growing up in Norristown, Pennsylvania," Spinelli notes. "Looking back now I can see that I was also gathering material that would one day find its way into my books." Spinelli uses humor to tell his stories. He has tackled tough topics such as racism, bullying, and sex.

Spinelli has written more than twenty books for young readers.

———

THE INSPIRATION FOR SPINELLI'S *THERE'S A GIRL IN MY HAMMERLOCK* CAME FROM A NEWSPAPER STORY HE READ ABOUT A GIRL WHO COMPETED ON HER HIGH SCHOOL WRESTLING TEAM.

He lives with his family in Phoenixville, Pennsylvania, where he continues to write.

✿

WHERE TO FIND OUT MORE ABOUT JERRY SPINELLI

BOOKS

Kovacs, Deborah, and James Preller. *Meet the Authors and Illustrators: 60 Creators of Favorite Children's Books Talk about Their Work.* Vol. 2. New York: Scholastic, 1993.

McGinty, Alice B. *Meet Jerry Spinelli.* New York: PowerKids Press, 2003.

McElmeel, Sharron L. *100 Most Popular Children's Authors: Biographical Sketches and Bibliographies.* Englewood, Colo.: Libraries Unlimited, 1999.

Spinelli, Jerry. *Knots in My Yo-Yo String. The Autobiography of a Kid.* New York: Knopf, 1998.

WEB SITES

THE AUTHOR CORNER
http://www.carr.lib.md.us/authco/spinelli-j.htm
For a short biography of and interview with Jerry Spinelli

EDUCATIONAL PAPERBACK ASSOCIATION
http://www.edupaperback.org/authorbios/Spinelli_Jerry.html
To learn more about Spinelli's work

HOUGHTON MIFFLIN MEET THE AUTHOR
http://www.eduplace.com/kids/hmr/mtai/spinelli.html
To read about Jerry Spinelli's life and books

————

SPINELLI BECAME A CHILDREN'S AUTHOR BY ACCIDENT. PUBLISHERS OF ADULT BOOKS WERE NOT INTERESTED IN *SPACE STATION SEVENTH GRADE* BECAUSE IT WAS ABOUT A THIRTEEN-YEAR-OLD. THEN A CHILDREN'S BOOK PUBLISHER LIKED THE BOOK AND PUBLISHED IT.

Diane Stanley

Born: December 27, 1943

Most of Diane Stanley's picture books are nonfiction. Sometimes they use beautiful, detailed illustrations to help tell the stories of people from history. Her best-known books include *Leonardo da Vinci, Cleopatra,* and *Peter the Great.*

Diane Stanley was born on December 27, 1943, in Abilene, Texas. Diane's parents divorced when she was very young. She lived in New York with her mother, Fay, who was an important part of her life. In fact, Diane Stanley believes it is because of her mother that she is an author today.

Fay Stanley took her daughter to museums and to the theater, and they read many books together. In fact, Fay Stanley helped Diane write

---

SOME OF STANLEY'S BOOKS WERE PUBLISHED UNDER
THE NAME DIANE ZUROMSKIS.

her first book! "She would type up my words, and I would draw the pictures," remembers Stanley. Fay Stanley herself wrote mystery books. From her mother's efforts, Diane saw that ordinary people could be successful authors if they liked words and worked hard.

Fay Stanley became very ill at one point, so Diane was sent back to Abilene to live with her aunt and uncle for several years. Then, she and her mother moved to La Jolla, California. When her mother became ill again, Diane returned to Texas and finished high school there.

After high school, Stanley attended Trinity University in San Antonio, Texas. She was interested in many things in college, including history and politics. But during her last year in college, she took an art course. "The teacher took me aside and told me he thought I had ability. That teacher changed the course of my life," notes Stanley. "I wonder how many teachers realize the power they have to mold the lives of their students?"

> *"Today, my life is all about books: writing them, illustrating them, reading them, and sharing them with children. I feel blessed."*

Then, Diane Stanley went to Johns Hopkins University, where she earned a master's degree in medical illustration. In 1970, she married and started work as a medical illustrator. She soon had two daughters.

Stanley read to her children as her mother had read to her. It was

STANLEY ILLUSTRATED A BOOK WRITTEN BY HER MOTHER. THE BOOK IS *THE LAST PRINCESS: THE STORY OF PRINCESS KA'IULANI OF HAWAI'I.*

A Selected Bibliography of Stanley's Work

Saladin: Noble Prince of Islam (2002)

Michaelangelo (2001)

A Time Apart (1999)

Peter the Great (1999)

Joan of Arc (1998)

Saving Sweetness (Text only, 1996)

Leonardo da Vinci (1996)

The True Adventure of Daniel Hall (1995)

Cleopatra (with Peter Vennema, 1994)

Charles Dickens: The Man Who Had Great Expectations (with Peter Vennema, 1993)

Moe the Dog in Tropical Paradise (1992)

Bard of Avon: The Story of William Shakespeare (with Peter Vennema, 1992)

The Last Princess: The Story of Princess Ka'iulani of Hawai'i (Illustrations only, 1991)

Good Queen Bess: The Story of Elizabeth I of England (with Peter Vennema, 1990)

Shaka: King of the Zulus (with Peter Vennema, 1988)

The Conversation Club (1983)

The Farmer in the Dell (Illustrations only, 1978)

Stanley's Major Literary Awards

2001 Orbis Pictus Honor Book
  Michaelangelo

1997 *Boston Globe–Horn Book* Nonfiction Honor Book
1997 Orbis Pictus Award
  Leonardo da Vinci

1992 Carter G. Woodson Book Award
  The Last Princess: The Story of Princess Ka'iulani of Hawai'i

1991 *Boston Globe–Horn Book* Nonfiction Honor Book
  Good Queen Bess: The Story of Elizabeth I of England

during this time that Stanley decided to write children's books. "I realized that what I really wanted to do was make books for children. It was the perfect combination of my love of words, art, and book design," says Stanley.

Diane Stanley carefully researches a topic before she begins to write. She reads hundreds of pages before she begins writing and illustrating. Stanley often writes about people in history and events that happened in faraway places. Stanley likes to travel to see the places for herself so she can add details to both the story and the pictures. Sometimes she researches the pictures as much as she does the story.

Stanley and her second husband, Peter Vennema, live in Houston, Texas, where she continues to write and illustrate books for children. "I have deeply enjoyed moving along the path I set out upon over twenty years ago. Part of the fun is not knowing where it will take me," Stanley explains.

> *"If the reader doesn't have a feeling for the world my subject lived in, the story won't really come to life."*

WHERE TO FIND OUT MORE ABOUT DIANE STANLEY

BOOKS

Holtze, Sally Holmes, ed. *Sixth Book of Junior Authors & Illustrators.* New York: H .W. Wilson Company, 1989.

WEB SITES

CHILDREN'S BOOK COUNCIL
http://www.cbcbooks.org/html/dianestanley.html
To learn what Stanley says about her work

DIANE STANLEY'S WEB SITE
http://www.dianestanley.com/
For information about Stanley's life and books

NATIONAL CENTER FOR CHILDREN'S ILLUSTRATED LITERATURE
http://www.nccil.org/exhibit/stanley.html
For a biography of Diane Stanley

STANLEY AND HER HUSBAND, PETER VENNEMA, HAVE WORKED TOGETHER ON SEVERAL BOOKS.

William Steig

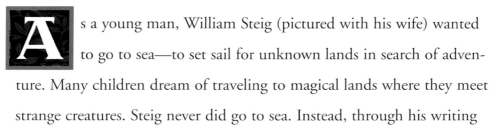

Born: November 14, 1907

As a young man, William Steig (pictured with his wife) wanted to go to sea—to set sail for unknown lands in search of adventure. Many children dream of traveling to magical lands where they meet strange creatures. Steig never did go to sea. Instead, through his writing

he launched more than thirty expeditions into the world of the imagination. His ships were his books, and his building materials were pictures and words. His books are filled with strange, sometimes ugly creatures made likable through their charm and goodness. They have sailed into the homes of children all over the world.

William Steig was familiar with painting from a young age. Born on November 14, 1907, in New York City, he had two parents

WILLIAM STEIG DIDN'T START WRITING FOR CHILDREN UNTIL HE WAS IN HIS SIXTIES, WHEN MOST ADULTS ARE THINKING ABOUT RETIREMENT.

who loved to paint. His father, Joseph, who was originally from Austria, worked as a house-painter to support the family. In his spare time, he joined his wife, Laura, at the easel, where the two painted for pleasure. William's brother Irwin became a professional painter. It was Irwin Steig who first gave William lessons on how to work colors on a palette and dab them on a canvas until the picture took on a life of its own.

In 1923, William Steig enrolled in the City College of

> *"Art, including juvenile literature, has the power to make any spot on earth the living center of the universe."*

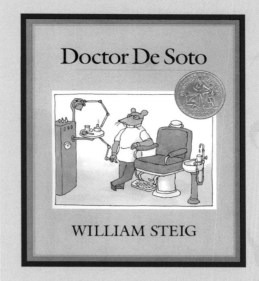

A Selected Bibliography of Steig's Work

Potch & Polly (2001)

Wizzil (2000)

Gift from Zeus: Sixteen Favorite Myths (Illustrations only, 2001)

Grown-Ups Get to Do All the Driving (1995)

Shrek! (1990)

Spinky Sulks (1988)

Doctor De Soto (1982)

Tiffky Doofky (1978)

Caleb & Kate (1977)

Abel's Island (1976)

The Amazing Bone (1976)

Dominic (1972)

Amos & Boris (1971)

Sylvester and the Magic Pebble (1969)

C D B (1968)

Steig's Major Literary Awards

1983 *Boston Globe–Horn Book* Picture Book Honor Book
1983 Newbery Honor Book
1982 American Book Award
   Doctor De Soto

1977 *Boston Globe–Horn Book* Picture Book Honor Book
1977 Caldecott Honor Book
   The Amazing Bone

1977 Newbery Honor Book
   Abel's Island

1970 Caldecott Medal
   Sylvester and the Magic Pebble

New York. After graduating, Steig sought professional art training at the National Academy of Design in New York City. Manhattan in the 1920s was a sea of dark-suited businessmen in dark hats. It was also a place filled with immigrants, who hoped to get rich in America. In short, it was a paradise for people who loved to watch people.

> *"I have a position—a point of view. But I don't have to think about it to express it. I can write about anything and my point of view will come out."*

Steig began to read the private struggles of these people on their faces. He observed the funny, sometimes absurd side of normal, everyday folks. He transformed these observations into cartoon drawings. He sold one of these cartoons to *The New Yorker,* a witty, intellectual New York magazine with a tradition of excellent cartoons. He has been contributing cartoons to the magazine ever since.

After almost forty years as a successful cartoonist, William Steig decided to try something new. He turned to children's fiction and illustration. His sense of comedy was transformed into adventure tales for children.

Steig's characters are pigs and mice who are often quite witty. They live in a world that feels safe, despite the presence of danger. Characters such as Shrek, a hideous green monster, are likable because they are

---

IN 2001, STEIG'S POPULAR BOOK *SHREK!* WAS TURNED INTO AN ANIMATED MOVIE THAT BECAME POPULAR WITH CHILDREN AND ADULTS.

funny and loyal to their friends. The lumpy Shrek is like an excitable version of sleepy Winnie-the-Pooh, and he captures the same innocent goodness. Steig's characters have found a vast audience of children hungry for intelligent entertainment.

❧

WHERE TO FIND OUT MORE ABOUT WILLIAM STEIG

BOOKS

Chevalier, Tracy, ed. *Twentieth-Century Children's Writers*. 3rd ed. Chicago: St. James Press, 1989.

Kovacs, Deborah, and James Preller. *Meet the Authors and Illustrators: 60 Creators of Favorite Children's Books Talk about Their Work*. Vol. 1. New York: Scholastic, 1991.

Lorenz, Lee, ed. *The World of William Steig*. New York: Artisan, 1998.

WEB SITES

EDUCATIONAL PAPERBACK ASSOCIATION
http://www.edupaperback.org/authorbios/Steig_William.html
To read a brief biography of Steig

KIDSREAD.COM
http://www.kidsreads.com/authors/au-steig-william.asp
For a biography of William Steig and related links

WILLIAM STEIG'S WEB SITE
http://www.williamsteig.com/
For a lot of information about William Steig

———

WILLIAM STEIG HAS PUBLISHED MORE THAN **1,600** CARTOONS IN *THE NEW YORKER* AND HAS DESIGNED **117** CARTOON COVERS FOR THE MAGAZINE.

John Steptoe

Born: September 14, 1950
Died: August 28, 1989

John Steptoe once said that the two greatest forces that shaped him were the outside world of New York City's streets and the inner world of his imagination. When he was sixteen years old, he combined these two worlds into the creation of a picture book entitled *Stevie.* It was published two years later in 1969. *Stevie* is about a boy named Robert trying to cope with the arrival of Stevie, a neighbor's child whom Robert's mother has agreed to look after. The remarkable thing about *Stevie* is that the characters speak the language that John Steptoe spoke growing up. The words are spelled out just as they would

JOHN STEPTOE WON ACCLAIM FOR HIS ADAPTATIONS OF NATIVE AMERICAN AND AFRICAN-AMERICAN FOLKTALES IN *THE STORY OF JUMPING MOUSE: A NATIVE AMERICAN LEGEND* AND *MUFARO'S BEAUTIFUL DAUGHTERS: AN AFRICAN TALE.*

be pronounced by black kids in the Bedford-Stuyvesant section of Brooklyn, New York, where Steptoe was raised. This style of writing in realistic dialogue had never really been done before.

John Steptoe was born on September 14, 1950, in Brooklyn. John was the oldest of four children. His father was a transit worker in New York City's subway system.

As a child, John Steptoe was amazed that no one in children's books spoke the way he did. The vast majority of

"Good books are more than a luxury; they are a necessary part of a child's development and it's all of our jobs to see that we all get them."

African-American children, he felt, were being ignored as readers.

John Steptoe started out as a painter, not a writer. He drew in the quiet of his home, while outside horns blared and throngs of people passed by. His talent won him a place at the High School of Art and Design in Manhattan. Just three months shy of finishing, he left school and New York, and started hitchhiking.

The hitchhiking didn't really lead anywhere, so Steptoe sent some of his pictures to New York publishers. *Stevie* was the result. After that, he produced many books that critics praised for their originality and for

JOHN STEPTOE'S COURAGE TO WRITE ABOUT SERIOUS THEMES FOR CHILDREN WON HIM MUCH ATTENTION. IN *DADDY IS A MONSTER . . . SOMETIMES*, HE WRITES ABOUT DOMESTIC PROBLEMS.

A Selected Bibliography of Steptoe's Work

Baby Says (1988)

Mufaro's Beautiful Daughters: An African Tale (1987)

The Story of Jumping Mouse: A Native American Legend (1984)

All the Colors of the Race: Poems (Illustrations only, 1982)

OUTside INside Poems (Illustrations only, 1981)

Mother Crocodile = Maman-Caïman (Illustrations only, 1981)

Daddy Is a Monster . . . Sometimes (1980)

She Come Bringing Me That Little Baby Girl (1974)

Train Ride (1971)

Uptown (1970)

Stevie (1969)

Steptoe's Major Literary Awards

1988 Caldecott Honor Book
1988 Coretta Scott King Illustrator Award
1987 *Boston Globe–Horn Book* Picture Book Award
   Mufaro's Beautiful Daughters: An African Tale

1985 Caldecott Honor Book
   The Story of Jumping Mouse: A Native American Legend

1983 Coretta Scott King Illustrator Honor Book
   All the Colors of the Race: Poems

1982 Coretta Scott King Illustrator Award
   Mother Crocodile = Maman-Caïman

1975 *Boston Globe–Horn Book* Picture Book Honor Book
   She Come Bringing Me That Little Baby Girl

taking on tough subjects. In *Train Ride,* for example, Steptoe depicts two young kids riding on the subway talking about what they want when they grow up. His drawings of the city include the graffiti that once decorated New York's subways. The children use the words of African-American city children, but the story is universal.

John Steptoe died on August 28, 1989, from AIDS-related complications. He was thirty-eight years old. Steptoe

"One of my incentives for getting into writing children's books was the great and disastrous need for books that black children could honestly relate to."

left behind a daughter, Bweela, and a son, Javaka. Javaka Steptoe followed in his father's footsteps by becoming a Coretta Sott King Award–winning illustrator.

❧

WHERE TO FIND OUT MORE ABOUT JOHN STEPTOE

BOOKS

Berg, Julie. *John Steptoe: The Young at Heart.*
Edina, Minn.: Abdo & Daughters, 1994.

De Montveville, Doris, and Elizabeth D. Crawford, eds.
Fourth Book of Junior Authors & Illustrators.
New York: H. W. Wilson Company, 1978.

Kovacs, Deborah, and James Preller. *Meet the Authors and Illustrators:*
60 Creators of Favorite Children's Books Talk about Their Work. Vol. 1.
New York: Scholastic, 1991.

WEB SITES

HALL KIDS TALES
http://hallkidstales.com/S/29.shtml
For a list of Steptoe's books with links to reviews and synopses

JOHN STEPTOE CHILDREN'S BOOKS
http://www.my-book-mall.com/Stevie_0064431223.html
For information about many of Steptoe's books

LEE & LOW BOOKTALK
http://www.leeandlow.com/booktalk/ teptoe.html
To read what Steptoe said about his work

IN 1989, JOHN STEPTOE'S *MUFARO'S BEAUTIFUL DAUGHTERS: AN AFRICAN TALE* WAS MADE INTO A MOTION PICTURE.

Janet Stevens

Born: January 17, 1953

Picture book author and illustrator Janet Stevens is a hit with kids and teachers alike. Kids love her zany, colorful drawings. In Stevens's books, readers might meet a bear in a Hawaiian shirt, a walrus in a tie, or an elephant in a tutu. Teachers love Stevens's work, too. They know that her wild and wacky illustrations excite kids and make them want to read.

Janet Stevens was born on January 17, 1953, in Dallas, Texas. She is the youngest of three kids. Her older brother and sister were good students in school, but Janet preferred to draw. In class, she doodled on all of her papers. Instead of writing book reports, she drew them. Janet's parents nicknamed her "the artist."

SOME OF STEVENS'S FAVORITE THINGS TO DRAW ARE SHOES WITH HIGH HEELS. SHE ALSO LIKES TO DRAW RHINOCEROSES, BEARS, PIGS, AND CATS.

In high school, Janet drew pictures for anything and anybody. She designed posters and yearbook covers. At the University of Colorado, she majored in art. During summer breaks, she flew to Honolulu and designed patterns for Hawaiian shirts! When Stevens graduated in 1975, she knew without a doubt that she wanted to be an artist.

In 1978, Stevens got her first job working on a children's book. That book was *Callooh! Callay!: Holiday Poems for Young Readers.* Since then, Stevens has worked full-time making books for kids. Sometimes she creates drawings for other people's books. She tries to put the author's vision into pictures. At

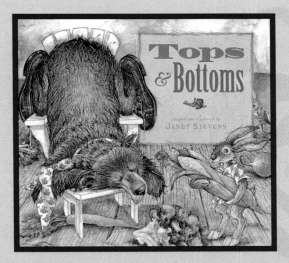

A Selected Bibliography of Stevens's Work

Epossumondas (Illustrations only, 2002)

Tumbleweed Stew (Illustrations only, 2000)

And the Dish Ran Away with the Spoon (with Susan Stevens Crummel, 2001)

Cook-a-Doodle-Doo! (with Susan Stevens Crummel, 1999)

My Big Dog (with Susan Stevens Crummel, 1999)

Shoe Town (with Susan Stevens Crummel, 1999)

To Market, to Market (Illustrations only, 1997)

Tops & Bottoms (1995)

Anansi and the Talking Melon (Illustrations only, 1994)

Coyote Steals the Blanket: An Ute Tale (1993)

Anansi Goes Fishing (Illustrations only, 1992)

The Dog Who Had Kittens (Illustrations only, 1991)

How the Manx Cat Lost Its Tail (1990)

Anansi and the Moss-Covered Rock (Illustrations only, 1988)

The Three Billy Goats Gruff (1987)

The Tortoise and the Hare: An Aesop Fable (1984)

The Princess and the Pea (1982)

Lucretia the Unbearable (Illustrations only, 1981)

Callooh! Callay!: Holiday Poems for Young Readers (Illustrations only, 1978)

Stevens's Major Literary Awards

1996 Caldecott Honor Book
Tops & Bottoms

"Each book is an opportunity and a challenge. A new book offers me a chance to expand and try something new. The process is both difficult and exciting—sometimes a struggle, sometimes fun. Most important is to create books that children want to read. This is the real joy of bookmaking."

other times, Stevens writes her own books or retells classic fables or fairy tales. When Stevens is working on her own book, she can let her imagination run wild.

Stevens is always looking for new ways to create art. In the past, she has used colored pencils, watercolors, and acrylic paints, as well as photo and fabric collages. Most recently, Stevens has begun creating art with her computer. She uses a scanner to take pictures of household items and store them in her computer. In *My Big Dog*, Stevens scanned in some cloth and buttons. Then she used the images of these items in her artwork.

Stevens's drawing style has also evolved over the years. She visits classrooms around the country and talks to kids about what they like to see. Stevens uses their comments to improve her work.

Stevens likes to include people she knows in her books. Her friends, family, and pets have all posed for her pictures. She also likes to draws things like furniture and shoes that are in her house. In *To Market! To Market!* Janet used the local grocery store as a model.

———

STEVENS AND HER SISTER, SUSAN STEVENS CRUMMEL, HAVE WRITTEN
A NUMBER OF CHILDREN'S BOOKS TOGETHER, INCLUDING *AND THE DISH RAN AWAY
WITH THE SPOON, COOK-A-DOODLE-DOO!, MY BIG DOG,* AND *SHOE TOWN.*

Janet Stevens lives in Boulder, Colorado, with her husband, son, daughter, three cats, and a dog. Stevens's two children are important to her work. They look at her books and tell her what they think. Stevens always tries to create

"Jump into a book like a cool swimming pool on a hot summer day, and feel it all around you. Read at your own pace. Reread the parts you don't get—or that you like the most. Dive into it! Become the character in the book; feel all the feelings."

drawings that her kids will enjoy, and she has certainly been successful.

WHERE TO FIND OUT MORE ABOUT JANET STEVENS

BOOKS

Holtze, Sally Holmes, ed. *Sixth Book of Junior Authors & Illustrators.*
New York: H .W. Wilson Company, 1989.

WEB SITES

JANET STEVENS'S WEB SITE
http://www.janetstevens.com/
For information about Janet Stevens's life and work

MEET JANET STEVENS
http://www.scottforesman.com/families/authors/stevens.html
To read an interview with Stevens

NATIONAL CENTER FOR CHILDREN'S ILLUSTRATED LITERATURE
http://www.nccil.org/exhibit/stevens.html
To learn more about Janet Stevens

WHEN JANET STEVENS WAS A CHILD, HER FATHER WAS IN THE NAVY, SO THE FAMILY MOVED AROUND A LOT. STEVENS HAS LIVED IN TEXAS, MASSACHUSETTS, MAINE, VIRGINIA, RHODE ISLAND, FLORIDA, HAWAII, GEORGIA, AND COLORADO.

R. L. Stine

Born: October 8, 1943

The writer most young readers think of when they think of scary books is R. L. Stine. But he is about as scary your local librarian. Far from having any ghoulish qualities, Stine is as friendly a guy as you'll ever meet. Just don't read his books if you're all alone in the house.

Robert Laurence Stine was born on October 8, 1943, in Columbus, Ohio. As a child, Stine read a great deal of science fiction. His favorite authors were Ray Bradbury and Isaac Asimov. He also loved old horror movies, as well as *Mad* magazine, and the comic books *Tales from the Crypt* and *The Vault of Horror*. These comics were both funny and scary at the same time. They would one day influence Stine's writing in the Goosebumps series.

R. L. Stine began writing at the age of nine. Using an old type-

WHAT SCARES R. L. STINE THE MOST? JUMPING INTO A SWIMMING POOL. ALTHOUGH HE CAN SWIM, HE SAYS HE HAS TO CLIMB, NOT JUMP, TO GET IN.

writer, he wrote joke books and short stories, and created his own magazines. He handed them out to his fellow students, much to the unhappiness of his teachers.

It was not until high school that R. L. Stine's teachers encouraged his writing, directing him to the high school newspaper, for

"I've liked scary stuff since I was a kid. My brother and I used to go to every scary movie that came out. We saw movies like It Came from beneath the Sea *and* The Creature from the Black Lagoon. *I remember these . . . when I think up titles for Goosebumps."*

which he wrote a regular humor column. After graduating from high school, Stine attended Ohio State University, where he was editor of the university's humor magazine, the *Sundial.*

Following college, he moved to New York City where he worked as a writer on books, magazines, and even a Nickelodeon television show called *Eureka's Castle.* Writing under the name Jovial Bob Stine, he wrote humor books such as *101 Silly Monster Jokes* and *Bozos on Patrol,* and he was the editor in chief of *Bananas,* a humor magazine for children.

In 1986 Stine wrote *Blind Date,* his first scary novel for teenagers. This was such a big hit that a few years later he began writing the Fear Street series of scary books for teenagers.

Then, in 1992, Stine launched Goosebumps, a new series of scary

———

R. L. Stine has his own pinball machine and pool table in his apartment in New York City. They help him relax following a hard day of writing.

57

Bad dog. Really BAD dog.

THE BARKING GHOST

A Selected Bibliography of Stine's Work

Beware!: R. L. Stine Picks His Favorite Scary Stories (2002)
The Howler (2001)
Dear Diary, I'm Dead (2000)
Locker 13 (2000)
Don't Forget Me! (2000)
Into the Twister of Terror (1999)
The Werewolf in the Living Room (1999)
Nightmare Hour (1999)
Fear Hall, the Beginning (1997)
The Girl Who Cried Monster (1997)
Go to Your Tomb—Right Now! (1997)
Beware of the Purple Peanut Butter (1996)
A Shocker on Shock Street (1995)
The New Boy (1994)
The Scarecrow Walks at Midnight (1994)
The Haunted Mask (1993)
The Secret (1993)
Be Careful What You Wish For . . . (1993)
Bozos on Patrol (1992)
Say Cheese and Die! (1992)
The Best Friend (1992)
Blind Date (1986)
101 Silly Monster Jokes (1986)

books for younger readers, ages eight to twelve. It went on to become the best-selling series of all time. Young readers loved the combination of horror and humor. The series, which still runs, has sold more than 200 million books and has been translated into sixteen languages in thirty-one countries.

Goosebumps became a successful TV series, but Stine never stopped writing books. (Working six days a week, Stine writes a new Goosebumps book and a new Fear Street book each month.) He has written one scary book for adults called *Superstitious,* but he says that he prefers writing for young readers.

R. L. Stine is proud that his writing has inspired many young people, especially boys who were not previously readers, to pick up books. He is dedicated to literacy for kids, and established a writing program in the middle school of his hometown, Columbus, Ohio. This "scary" writer with a sharp sense of humor says

"My advice is to read, read, read. And don't just read me, read all kinds of authors. That way, you pick up a lot of different writing styles. . . . If you're really serious about writing, you should write something every day, even if it's just a paragraph."

that on his tombstone he wants the words: "He got boys to read."

WHERE TO FIND OUT MORE ABOUT R. L. STINE

BOOKS

Cohen, Joel H. *R. L. Stine*. Minneapolis: Lucent Books, 2000.

Meister, Cari. *R. L. Stine*. Edina, Minn.: Abdo & Daughters, 2002.

Stine, R. L., and Joe Arthur. *It Came from Ohio: My Life As a Writer*. New York: Scholastic, 1997.

WEB SITES

GOOSEBUMPS
http://www.scholastic.com/goosebumps/
To learn more about the Goosebumps series

THE NIGHTMARE ROOM
http://www.thenightmareroom.com/
To see R. L. Stine's Web site

SCIENCE-FICTION GREAT RAY BRADBURY'S NOVEL *SOMETHING WICKED THIS WAY COMES* IS STINE'S FAVORITE SCARY BOOK. HE CALLS IT THE MOST FRIGHTENING BOOK HE'S EVER READ!

Mildred D. Taylor

Born: September 13, 1943

Mildred D. Taylor noticed something odd about the children's books that she read as a child: No one looked like her. African-Americans were absent from the books she read. Even at school when she learned about slavery and the history of black America, she wondered where the heroes were. Were there no blacks who stood up for their rights? Were there no black families full of love and compassion?

Of course there were, and Mildred Taylor spent a good part of her career writing about one such African-Americans family called the Logans. Taylor depicts the same humor and struggles that all families go through in her Logan stories. But she also captures the unique struggle of growing up black in America.

IN 1978, MILDRED D. TAYLOR'S *ROLL OF THUNDER, HEAR MY CRY* WAS PRODUCED AS A MINISERIES FOR **ABC** TELEVISION. THE BOOK ALSO WON A NEWBERY MEDAL IN 1977.

Mildred Taylor was born in Jackson, Mississippi, on September 13, 1943, at a time when open hatred of blacks could be found all over America. Prejudice was written into the law. In the South, blacks lived a separate existence from whites. They rode in different sections of the bus and dined in different restaurants. Blacks feared a run-in with the law because the police did not treat them fairly.

"When we children had finished all the games we could think to play, we would join the adults, . . . for it would often turn to . . . a history of black people told through stories."

A Selected Bibliography of Taylor's Work

The Land (2001)
Mississippi Bridge (1990)
The Road to Memphis (1990)
The Friendship (1987)
The Gold Cadillac (1987)
Let the Circle Be Unbroken (1981)
Roll of Thunder, Hear My Cry (1976)
Song of the Trees (1975)

Taylor's Major Literary Awards

2002 Coretta Scott King Author Award
    The Land

1991 Coretta Scott King Author Award
    The Road to Memphis

1988 *Boston Globe–Horn Book* Fiction Award
1988 Coretta Scott King Author Award
    The Friendship

1982 Coretta Scott King Author Award
    Let the Circle Be Unbroken

1977 *Boston Globe–Horn Book* Fiction Honor Book
1977 Newbery Medal
    Roll of Thunder, Hear My Cry

When African-Americans history was mentioned in class, Mildred found it to be a sad tale. Blacks were represented as helpless victims of slavery and prejudice. They somehow didn't come across as humans, with regular feelings and pride in their history.

Taylor attended college in Toledo, Ohio. She later earned a master's degree in journalism at the University of Colorado. Taylor attended school in the 1960s, when black students were fighting to end racist laws.

Taylor's interest in black history led her to work in Ethiopia as a Peace Corps volunteer. For two years, she taught English and history. When she returned to the United States in 1967, she trained other Peace Corps recruits.

> *"It is my hope that to the children who read my books, the Logans will provide those heroes missing from the schoolbooks of my childhood, Black men, women, and children of whom they can be proud."*

After moving to Los Angeles in 1971, Taylor started a novel about a black family in the South during the Great Depression. When she finished writing *Song of the Trees,* Taylor submitted it to the Council of Interracial Books for Children in 1974—and won first prize!

Since then, Mildred D. Taylor has written several novels about the Logans, including *Roll of Thunder, Hear My Cry,* which won a Newbery Medal. Taylor's books capture the struggle for dignity in a

----

TAYLOR HAS CALLED HER FATHER A "MASTER STORYTELLER." IN FACT, SHE INCLUDED MANY OF HER FAMILY'S REAL-LIFE STORIES IN HER NOVELS.

country that proclaimed equality—but only for whites. In Taylor's world, the struggle is always dignified, and being African-American is something to be proud of.

Mildred D. Taylor lives in Colorado. She continues to write novels for young people.

❧

WHERE TO FIND OUT MORE ABOUT MILDRED D. TAYLOR

BOOKS

Crowe, Chris. *Presenting Mildred Taylor.*
New York: Twayne Publications, 1999.

Drew, Bernard A. *The 100 Most Popular Young Adult Authors.*
Englewood, Colo.: Libraries Unlimited, 1997

Kovacs, Deborah, and James Preller. *Meet the Authors and Illustrators:*
60 Creators of Favorite Children's Books Talk about Their Work. Vol. 1.
New York: Scholastic, 1991.

Rediger, Pat. *Great African Americans in Literature.*
New York: Crabtree, 1996.

WEB SITES

HOOKED ON BOOKS
http://www.kidlink.org/KIDPROJ/Books/reviews.html
For reviews of Taylor's books, all written by kids

LET THE CIRCLE BE UNBROKEN
http://www.ced.appstate.edu/whs/letcircl.htm
For a review and analysis of the book

―――

MILDRED D. TAYLOR'S MIDDLE NAME—AND FAMILY NICKNAME—IS DELOIS.

Sydney Taylor

Born: 1904
Died: February 12, 1978

S ydney Taylor grew up on New York City's Lower East Side in the early days of the twentieth century. Her experiences there inspired much of her writing.

She was born in 1904 to an immigrant Jewish family, the middle daughter of six children—five girls and one boy. In those days, the crowded tenement houses of the Lower East Side were filled with immigrants. Taylor later called it "in many ways an extension of the ghettos in middle Europe." It was a hard but exciting place to grow up. Taylor said that though the neighborhood was filled with poverty, sickness, hard work, and long hours, it also had the joy of freedom and opportunity.

> *"When I was a little girl and people asked, 'What would you like to be when you grow up?' I used to answer, 'An author.' But when I grew up, life had so many other attractions, I forgot about my first ambition."*

THE FIVE ALL-OF-A-KIND FAMILY STORIES ALL TAKE PLACE DURING FIVE YEARS IN THE EARLY TWENTIETH CENTURY. BUT IT TOOK TAYLOR MORE THAN TWENTY-FIVE YEARS TO WRITE THEM ALL.

Though Sydney and her family were poor, she knew they were lucky. Most families near them lived in five-story tenement buildings with no elevators and no hot water or heat. Sydney's family lived in a two-story house. And though their apartment still didn't have heat, they had their own bathroom and didn't have to share it with other families.

Taylor went to New York University, which was not far from her home. She studied drama. After graduating, she got a job as a secretary and spent her evenings working as an actress with a theater troupe called the Lenox Hill Players. She had a moment of glory with the group—one time the leading lady got sick and Taylor got to

A Selected Bibliography of Taylor's Work

Danny Loves a Holiday (1980)
Ella of All-of-a-Kind Family (1978)
All-of-a-Kind Family Downtown (1972)
A Papa Like Everyone Else (1966)
The Dog Who Came to Dinner (1966)
Mr. Barney's Beard (1961)
All-of-a-Kind Family Uptown (1958)
More All-of-a-Kind Family (1954)
All-of-a-Kind Family (1951)

play her part for two nights on Broadway. As part of her work with the theater, Taylor learned to dance. She became interested in dancing and performed in the Martha Taylor Dance Company from 1930 to 1935.

Taylor got married in 1925 and had a daughter named Jo. "Jo, being an only child, would listen avidly as I'd tell her about my mama, papa, and the five little sisters who lived on New York's Lower East Side," Taylor recalled later. "In the retelling, I suddenly felt a great compulsion to write it all down." That story was filled with the details of life at the turn of the century. Taylor remembered the Jewish customs and the Yiddish phrases she used to hear. She put it all on paper and let Jo and her friends read it. Then she lost interest. She stuck the story in a box and forgot about it.

Her husband didn't forget it. Starting in the 1940s, Taylor spent the summers teaching drama and dance at a camp. One summer while Taylor was gone, her husband got the story out and entered it in a contest for children's books. When Taylor returned, she got a big surprise. An editor at Follett Books contacted her,

> *"Our family was but a drop in the stream of bustling excitement and riotous color of the East Side of my memory. Immigrants from many lands poured into its narrow streets, bringing with them their firm beliefs in their destiny, their love of family, their great respect for learning, and . . . their hope for a better future in America."*

TAYLOR RARELY TESTED HER IDEAS OUT ON CHILDREN. "I FEEL THEY ARE IMPRESSED TOO MUCH BY ONE'S MANNER OR PRESENTATION," SHE EXPLAINED.

telling her she had won and asking to publish the story!

That book, *All-of-a-Kind Family,* was published in 1951. It was successful and became the first of a series that included *More All-of-a-Kind Family, All-of-a-Kind Family Uptown, All-of-a-Kind Family Downtown,* and *Ella of All-of-a-Kind Family.* She also wrote several books for very young readers. Sydney Taylor died on February 12, 1978.

WHERE TO FIND OUT MORE ABOUT SYDNEY TAYLOR

BOOKS
Fuller, Muriel, ed. *More Junior Authors.*
New York: H. W. Wilson Company, 1963.

WEB SITES
LOGANBERRY BOOKS
http://www.logan.com/loganberry/most-taylor.html
For a selection of Taylor's books

THE SYDNEY TAYLOR BOOK AWARD
http://www.jewishlibraries.org/ajlweb/awardsscholarships_files/taylor_book.htm
To learn more about the award established in Taylor's name

AFTER TAYLOR DIED IN 1978, HER HUSBAND STARTED AN AWARD
IN HER NAME FOR THE BEST JEWISH CHILDREN'S FICTION. THE AWARD IS
STILL GIVEN BY THE ASSOCIATION OF JEWISH LIBRARIES.

J. R. R. Tolkien

Born: January 3, 1892
Died: September 2, 1973

J. R. R. Tolkien created his own world filled with strange characters. His books tell the story of a fantasy world called Middle-earth where readers meet hobbits, elves, dwarfs, and orcs. Tolkien is best known as the author of *The Hobbit; or, There and Back Again* and The Lord of the Rings trilogy. His books were written decades ago yet remain popular with young readers.

John Ronald Reuel (J. R. R.) Tolkien was born on January 3, 1892, in Bloemfontein, South Africa, where his father was a bank manager. When Ronald was three, his mother took him and his brother back to England. His father stayed in South Africa, planning to join his family later. Ronald's father died in 1896, however, before he could move back to England. Ronald's mother was left to raise Ronald and his brother by herself.

IN 2002, A FIRST EDITION OF *THE HOBBIT* SOLD FOR MORE THAN $60,000. IT WAS THE HIGHEST PRICE EVER PAID FOR A TOLKIEN BOOK.

Ronald's mother introduced him to reading, writing, and her love of words. She also encouraged her sons to have a strong faith in the Catholic Church.

When Ronald was about twelve years old, his mother died of diabetes. Before her death, she arranged for Father Francis Xavier Morgan, a Catholic priest, to be her children's guardian. Father Morgan raised the boys, taught them a great deal, and helped pay for their education.

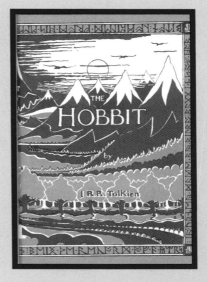

A Selected Bibliography of Tolkien's Work

Roverandom (1999)
The Silmarillion (with Christopher Tolkien, 1977)
The Father Christmas Letters (1976)
The Return of the King (1955)
The Fellowship of the Ring (1954)
The Two Towers (1954)
Farmer Giles of Ham (1949)
The Hobbit; or, There and Back Again (1937)

"If you really want to know what Middle-earth is based on, it's my wonder and delight in the earth as it is, particularly the natural earth."

As a student, Ronald loved the study of languages. Like many students at the time, he learned Latin and Greek. He also taught himself to speak and write several other languages.

> *"I had the habit while my children were still young of inventing and telling orally, sometimes of writing down, 'children's stories' for their private amusement.* The Hobbit *was intended to be one of them."*

Tolkien was a student at Oxford University when he began writing. After serving in the army in World War I (1914–1918), he took a job working with the *Oxford English Dictionary* for about two years. He then went on to become a professor of English at Oxford University.

Tolkien began writing *The Hobbit; or, There and Back Again* while teaching at Oxford. It was published in 1937 and was a great success. Later that same year, he began writing another book as a sequel to *The Hobbit.*

It took Tolkien more than eleven years to finish The Lord of the Rings trilogy. He was busy with his teaching schedule, but he rewrote parts of the story many times. The first two parts of the trilogy, *The Fellowship of the Ring* and *The Two Towers,* were published in 1954. The third part, *The Return of the King,* was not released until late 1955. The Lord of the Rings trilogy was a financial success for Tolkien and was translated into many languages.

THE THREE VOLUMES OF THE THE LORD OF THE RINGS HAVE BEEN ADAPTED INTO MOTION PICTURES. THE FIRST FILM, *THE FELLOWSHIP OF THE RING,* WAS RELEASED IN 2001.

Tolkien's books continue to be popular today. His stories have been adapted for television and motion pictures.

J. R. R. Tolkien died on September 2, 1973, in England. He was eighty-one years old.

WHERE TO FIND OUT MORE ABOUT J. R. R. TOLKIEN

BOOKS

Becker, Alida, ed. *The Tolkien Scrapbook.*
Philadelphia: Running Press, 1978.

Hammond, Wayne G., and Christina Scull, eds.
J. R. R. Tolkien: Artist and Illustrator.
Boston: Houghton Mifflin, 2000.

Niemark, Anne E., and Brad Weinman, ill.
Myth Maker: J. R. R. Tolkien.
New York: Harcourt, 1996.

WEB SITES

THE TOLKIEN SOCIETY
http://www.tolkiensociety.org/index.html
An extensive site dedicated to J. R. R. Tolkien

THE TOLKIEN TIMELINE
http://gollum.usask.ca/tolkien/
For a chronology of important events in J. R. R. Tolkien's life

AT THE TIME OF HIS DEATH, TOLKIEN WAS WORKING ON HIS BOOK *THE SILMARILLION.* HIS SON CHRISTOPHER COMPLETED THE BOOK AND PUBLISHED IT FOUR YEARS LATER.

P. L. Travers

Born: August 9, 1899
Died: April 23, 1996

Who wouldn't want to be raised by Mary Poppins? She is magical and marvelous, stern and tender, secretive and proud, and more than a little bit vain. To millions of children around the world, Mary Poppins is the ultimate British nanny.

Mary Poppins is the creation of Pamela Lyndon Travers, who was born Helen Lyndon Goff in Queensland, Australia, on August 9, 1899. As a child, Helen loved fairy tales and magic. "I shall never know," Travers once wrote, "which good lady it was who, at my own christening, gave me the everlasting gift, spotless amid all spotted joys, of love for the fairy tale."

Whether it was because of a fairy godmother or her own story-telling parents, Helen grew up reading and writing poems and stories. In

A STATUE OF MARY POPPINS STANDS IN NEW YORK CITY'S CENTRAL PARK. P. L. TRAVERS POSED FOR IT IN 1963.

her grown-up years, Travers would say that she couldn't remember a time when she didn't write. Writing—mostly fairy tales about magical beings—came as naturally to her as breathing.

Even more than writing, Helen loved theater. She loved everything about the stage— writing plays, acting in plays, and producing plays. She was always involved in her school's theatrical productions, and she performed in

> *"Mary Poppins's chief characteristic, apart from her tremendous vanity, is that she never explains. I often wonder why people write and ask me to explain this and that. I'll write back and say that Mary Poppins didn't explain, so neither can I or neither will I."*

her first "real" play when she was only ten.

By then, Helen and her mother and two younger sisters were living on a sugar plantation in New South Wales with her great-aunt Sass. Her father had died when she was only seven—the first great sorrow of her life. But Aunt Sass stepped in to take care of the family. She became part of the inspiration for Mary Poppins.

As she grew older, Helen (who took the stage name Pamela Lynden Travers) continued acting and writing. She worked with traveling Shake-spearean companies when she was a teenager and had her first poems published when she was just sixteen.

TRAVERS GUARDED HER PRIVACY WITH GREAT CARE. AFTER WRITING
MARY POPPINS, SHE SIGNED HER BOOKS WITH HER INITIALS ONLY.
USING HER INITIALS SEEMED ONE WAY TO HIDE HERSELF.

Mary Poppins

P. L. Travers

A Selected Bibliography of Travers's Work

Friend Monkey (1971)
I Go by Sea, I Go by Land (1964)
Mary Poppins in the Park (1952)
Mary Poppins Opens the Door (1943)
Aunt Sass (1941)
Mary Poppins Comes Back (1935)
Mary Poppins (1934)

But Travers wanted more. Carefully saving the money she earned from acting, she soon had enough to travel to Great Britain. This was where her mother and father came from. To Travers, it felt like home.

Travers was talented and lucky, and she soon found work as a journalist. She also published poems in the *Irish Statesman,* a famous literary magazine, and became friends with some of the best writers of the time.

Travers earned her own fame when she published *Mary Poppins* in 1934. She wrote the book in an old thatched house in the English countryside, while she was recovering from a long illness. Friends insisted that she send the story to a publisher—and the rest is history.

Travers wrote a number of sequels about Mary Poppins and the Banks children she cares for so primly, magically, and lovingly. The Mary Poppins titles are still beloved by millions of children all around the world. P. L. Travers died in London, England, on April 23, 1996.

> *"I think the idea of Mary Poppins has been blowing in and out of me, like a curtain at a window, all my life. My sister assures me that I told her stories of Mary Poppins when we were very small children."*

WHERE TO FIND OUT MORE ABOUT P. L. TRAVERS

BOOKS

Demers, Patricia. *P. L. Travers.* New York: Twayne Publications, 1991.

Draper, Ellen Dooling, and Jenny Koralek, eds. *A Lively Oracle: A Centennial Celebration of P. L. Travers, Creator of Mary Poppins.* Burdett, N.Y.: Larson Publications, 1999.

Lawson, Valerie. *Out of the Sky She Came.* London: Hodder Headline Group, 1999.

WEB SITES

FANTASTIC FICTION
http://www.fantasticfiction.co.uk/authors/P_L_Travers.htm
For information about Travers's writing

HALL KIDS
http://hallkidstales.com/T/9.shtml
To learn about Travers's most popular books

———

ONE OF TRAVERS'S FAVORITE CHILDHOOD GAMES INVOLVED MAKING A NEST IN THE FIELD OF WEEDS ALONGSIDE HER HOUSE AND PRETENDING SHE WAS A BIRD LAYING EGGS. HER MOTHER PLAYED RIGHT ALONG WITH HER!

Chris Van Allsburg

Born: June 18, 1949

Chris Van Allsburg is best known for the mysterious feelings in the stories he writes and in the beautiful illustrations he creates for them. Sometimes Van Allsburg makes bizarre events look believable. In *Jumanji,* a herd of rhinoceroses charges into a family's living room and pythons appear above the fireplace, but Van Allsburg draws the scene so it looks almost normal. On the other hand, the artist knows how to make even the most ordinary scene look odd—as if something strange is going on. "Think of it this way," Van Allsburg says, "the style I use allows me to make a drawing that has a little mystery to it, even if the actual things I am drawing are not strange or mysterious."

This quality has helped make Van Allsburg one of the best-known children's illustrators. He has twice won the Caldecott Medal,

VAN ALLSBURG SAYS KIDS AREN'T ON HIS MIND WHEN HE WRITES HIS BOOKS. "WHEN I SET OUT TO TELL A STORY, I'M JUST TRYING TO INTEREST MYSELF," HE EXPLAINS.

one of the highest awards for picture books. *Jumanji* was made into a movie. And his book *The Polar Express* is found in more libraries than almost any other children's book.

Chris Van Allsburg was born on June 18, 1949, in Grand Rapids, Michigan. He says he did "normal kid things," while he was growing up— catching tadpoles, playing baseball, and building model planes and trucks. He attended the University of Michigan where two important things happened to him: He met Lisa Morrison, the woman he would marry, while teaching her how to use a power saw in an art class. And he discovered that he wanted to be an artist.

A Selected Bibliography of Van Allsburg's Work

Zathura: A Space Adventure (2002)
The Veil of Snows (Illustrations only, 1997)
A City in Winter (Illustrations only, 1996)
Just a Dream (1990)
The Alphabet Theatre Proudly Presents the Z Was Zapped: A Play in Twenty-Six Acts (1987)
The Stranger (1986)
The Polar Express (1985)
The Mysteries of Harris Burdick (1984)
The Wreck of the Zephyr (1983)
Ben's Dream: Story and Pictures (1982)
Jumanji (1981)
The Garden of Abdul Gasazi (1979)

Van Allsburg's Major Literary Awards

1986 *Boston Globe–Horn Book* Picture Book Honor Book
1986 Caldecott Medal
　　The Polar Express

1985 *Boston Globe–Horn Book* Picture Book Honor Book
　　The Mysteries of Harris Burdick

1982 Caldecott Medal
1981 *Boston Globe–Horn Book* Picture Book Honor Book
　　Jumanji

1980 *Boston Globe–Horn Book* Picture Book Award
1980 Caldecott Honor Book
　　The Garden of Abdul Gasazi

After college, Van Allsburg continued to study art at the Rhode Island School of Design (where he was also a teacher for more than ten years). He was mostly interested in sculpture and exhibited his work at important museums and galleries.

> *"The first book I remember reading [was about] Dick, Jane, and Spot. Actually, the lives of this trio were not all that interesting. A young reader's reward for struggling through those syllables at the bottom of the page was to discover that Spot got a bath. Not exactly an exciting revelation."*

Van Allsburg's wife persuaded him to try his hand at a children's book. His first story, *The Garden of Abdul Gasazi,* was published in 1979. It is about a dog that escapes into a magician's garden and (maybe) gets turned into a duck. The book was a success.

Van Allsburg's second book, *Jumanji,* was an even greater success, winning him his first Caldecott Medal. The story, about a board game that causes magical problems in the home of two bored children, was later made into a movie starring Robin Williams. In 1983 came *The Wreck of the Zephyr,* Van Allsburg's first book in color. And in 1985, Van Allsburg published *The Polar Express,* his very popular Christmas fable.

Van Allsburg has written close to twenty books for children, including *The Alphabet Theatre Proudly Presents the Z Was Zapped: A Play in Twenty-Six Acts.* Some of his books include interesting experiments. For

IN A SPECIAL ANNIVERSARY EDITION OF *THE POLAR EXPRESS,* VAN ALLSBURG ADDED AN INTRODUCTION EXPLAINING THAT HE STOLE THE STORY FROM A BEGGAR CHILD ONE COLD NIGHT. SOME PEOPLE DIDN'T REALIZE VAN ALLSBURG WAS JOKING.

instance, *The Mysteries of Harris Burdick* consists of a set of strange illustrations. The book says that the story has been lost and readers will have to make up their own.

Van Allsburg lives and works in an old house in Providence, Rhode Island. He and his wife have two daughters.

> *"I create a story by posing questions to myself. I call it the 'what if' and 'what then' approach. For example, for my book* Jumanji, *I started out by thinking 'What if two bored children discovered a board game? What if the board game came to life? What then?'"*

⁊

WHERE TO FIND OUT MORE ABOUT CHRIS VAN ALLSBURG

BOOKS

Kovacs, Deborah, and James Preller. *Meet the Authors and Illustrators: 60 Creators of Favorite Children's Books Talk about Their Work.* Vol. 1. New York: Scholastic, 1991.

Palumbo, Tom. *Integrating the Literature of Chris Van Allsburg in the Classroom.* New York: McGraw-Hill Children's Publishing, 1996.

WEB SITES

ASK THE AUTHOR
http://www.eduplace.com/rdg/author/cva/question.html
To read an interview with Chris Van Allsburg

HOUGHTON MIFFLIN BOOKS
http://www.houghtonmifflinbooks.com/authors/vanallsburg/
For information about the world of Chris Van Allsburg

———

IN 1997, THE U.S. POSTAL SERVICE ISSUED A STAMP DESIGNED BY VAN ALLSBURG. THE THIRTY-TWO-CENT "HELPING CHILDREN LEARN" STAMP SHOWS A FATHER AND DAUGHTER READING TOGETHER.

Judith Viorst

Born: February 2, 1931

For more than thirty years, Judith Viorst has been reaching out to people of all ages through her writing. She has written everything from children's fiction and nonfiction to adult poetry and self-help books. Her best-loved books, though, are the ones she wrote about her own family. Young readers appreciate Viorst's honesty. She creates characters—kids and adults alike—who are not perfect and very human. Her stories help readers laugh at the problems that go along with being a kid.

Judith Viorst was born on February 2, 1931 in Newark, New Jersey. Even at an early age, Judith knew that she wanted to be a writer. One of the first things she ever wrote was a poem about her parents. As she grew

<hr>

VIORST'S PICTURE BOOKS TAKE SEVERAL MONTHS TO WRITE. HER CHILDREN'S POETRY BOOKS TAKE ABOUT TWO YEARS.

older, Judith continued writing poetry and stories about her life. She used her feelings as fuel for her writing. Although she tried to get her work published, she was not successful.

After Viorst graduated from college, she moved to Greenwich Village in New York City. There she began her career in publishing, first as a secretary for a magazine. After she was married, Viorst moved to Washington, D.C. In Washing-

> *"I like to take all my feelings and thoughts and put them down in different ways on paper."*

ton, she worked as an editor of science books. This gave Viorst her first chance to write for kids. From 1962 to 1967, she published four science books for teens.

Viorst decided to try her hand at writing fiction when her three sons were growing up. Like other kids, Anthony, Nicholas, and Alexander had their share of day-to-day problems. Viorst wrote stories that she thought might help them—or at least might make them smile. The first book about her boys was *Sunday Morning: A Story,* published in 1968. *Sunday Morning* features two overactive youngsters named Anthony and Nick. Other books about Viorst's sons cover such topics as sibling rivalry, the death of a pet, and very bad days.

Viorst's most popular book for kids is *Alexander and the Terrible, Horrible, No Good, Very Bad Day.* The book was written in 1972, about

---

JUDITH VIORST'S HUSBAND, MILTON, IS A POLITICAL WRITER WHO HAS COVERED THE MIDDLE EAST FOR MANY YEARS.

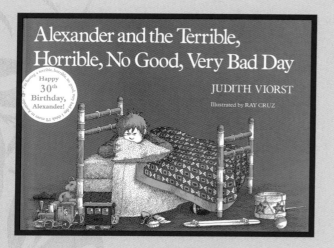

Alexander and the Terrible, Horrible, No Good, Very Bad Day

JUDITH VIORST

Illustrated by RAY CRUZ

Happy 30th Birthday, Alexander!

A Selected Bibliography of Viorst's Work

Super-Completely and Totally the Messiest (2000)

Alexander Who's Not (Do You Hear Me? I Mean It!) Going to Move (1995)

Sad Underwear and Other Complications: More Poems for Children and Their Parents (1995)

The Alphabet from Z to A: (With Much Confusion on the Way) (1993)

Earrings! (1990)

The Good-Bye Book (1988)

If I Were in Charge of the World and Other Worries: Poems for Children and Their Parents (1981)

Alexander, Who Used to Be Rich Last Sunday (1978)

Rosie and Michael (1974)

My Mama Says There Aren't Any Zombies, Ghosts, Vampires, Creatures, Demons, Monsters, Fiends, Goblins, or Things (1973)

Alexander and the Terrible, Horrible, No Good, Very Bad Day (1972)

The Tenth Good Thing about Barney (1971)

Try It Again, Sam; Safety When You Walk (1970)

I'll Fix Anthony (1969)

Sunday Morning: A Story (1968)

Viorst's youngest son. Since it was published, the book has sold more than two million copies. Kids today still enjoy reading about Alexander's mishaps. In 1998, the book was made into a musical play, and Viorst wrote the lyrics. *Alexander* opened to rave reviews at the Kennedy Center in Washington, D.C., and later toured around the nation.

As her boys grew older, Viorst turned her attention to other kinds of writing. She has written books of poetry for kids and adults. She is well known by

"The writing of [children's books] gives me enormous joy and satisfaction."

many adult readers for her humorous books about getting older. She has also written serious books for adults about marriage and grief. Viorst writes articles and columns for various magazines and newspapers, too.

Although her sons have all grown up and moved out of the house, Judith Viorst still writes for children from time to time. She has said that she hopes to keep writing children's books for as long as she lives.

❧

WHERE TO FIND OUT MORE ABOUT JUDITH VIORST

BOOKS

Mote, Dave. *Contemporary Popular Writers.* 1st ed. Detroit: St. James Press, 1996.

Wheeler, Jill C. *Judith Viorst.* Edina, Minn.: Abdo & Daughters, 1997.

WEB SITES

BOOK REPORTER
http://www.bookreporter.com/brc/author.asp?author=388
For an interview with and further information about Viorst

EDUCATIONAL PAPERBACK ASSOCIATION
http://www.edupaperback.org/authorbios/Viorst_Judith.html
For information about Viorst's life and work

KENNEDY CENTER
http://kennedy-center.org/programs/family/alexander/author.html
To read a short biography of and an interview with Viorst

JUDITH VIORST'S CHILDREN'S BOOKS HAVE BEEN TRANSLATED INTO MANY LANGUAGES, INCLUDING DUTCH, FRENCH, GERMAN, JAPANESE, AND SPANISH.

Cynthia Voigt

Born: February 25, 1942

Cynthia Voigt read a lot as a child. She liked reading series books such as Nancy Drew mysteries and Cherry Ames. Most of the books she enjoyed were given to her by her parents. When she found a copy of the children's classic *The Secret Garden* by Frances Hodgson Burnett at her grandmother's house, she not only loved the story, but was thrilled by the feeling of discovering a book all by herself. This thrill of

discovery would carry over to her work as a teacher and a children's book author.

Cynthia Voigt was born on February 25, 1942, in Boston, Massachusetts. Her mother's name was Elise Keeney, and her father, a corporate executive, was Frederick C. Irving. Young Cynthia Irving was the second of four children. The family moved to Connecticut when she was in elementary school, and Cynthia had a fairly happy childhood.

ON TRIPS TO THE LIBRARY TO FIND BOOKS FOR HER FIFTH-GRADE STUDENTS, VOIGT WOULD SOMETIMES CHECK OUT AS MANY AS THIRTY BOOKS IN ONE DAY.

By the time she entered high school, Cynthia was aiming for a career as a writer. She loved reading, and she got a thrill out of making up her own stories. After graduating from Smith College in Massachusetts, she went to St. Michael's College in Santa Fe, New Mexico, for her graduate work.

Voight was working at an advertising agency in New York City when she got married in 1964. She and her new husband soon moved to Sante Fe. In college, Voigt had vowed never to be a teacher. But in Santa Fe, she

"I enjoy almost everything I do, perhaps because when I don't enjoy something, I don't do it."

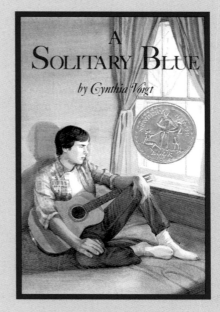

A Selected Bibliography of Voigt's Work

Elske (1999)
Bad Girls (1996)
The Wings of a Falcon (1993)
Orfe (1992)
David and Jonathan (1991)
Glass Mountain: A Novel (1991)
Seventeen against the Dealer (1989)
Sons from Afar (1987)
Come a Stranger (1986)
Izzy, Willy-Nilly (1986)
Stories about Rosie (1986)
Jackaroo (1985)
The Runner (1985)
Building Blocks (1984)
The Callender Papers (1983)
A Solitary Blue (1983)
Dicey's Song (1982)
Homecoming (1981)

Voigt's Major Literary Awards

1984 *Boston Globe–Horn Book* Fiction Honor Book
1984 Newbery Honor Book
   A Solitary Blue

1983 *Boston Globe–Horn Book* Fiction Honor Book
1983 Newbery Medal
   Dicey's Song

began teaching fourth and fifth grade, and she quickly discovered that she loved teaching.

Voigt's plans to become a writer were put on hold while she raised her children. After her divorce in 1972, she moved to Maryland, got a teaching job, and decided to try her hand at writing for children. Establishing a regular routine of writing for a minimum of one hour a day, Voigt began working on her first book, *Homecoming.*

"I always wanted to be a writer, always from the age of twelve. Even earlier than that I was a reader. I love a good story, and I love to meet interesting characters, and I like thinking."

After she remarried in 1974, Voigt decided to teach only part time, so she could dedicate more time to her writing. *Homecoming,* which introduced the character of Dicey Tillerman, was published in 1981.

Cynthia Voigt's second book about the Tillermans, *Dicey's Song,* won the 1983 Newbery Medal and established her as an important voice in children's literature. *Dicey's Song* tells of how thirteen-year-old Dicey Tillerman takes care of her younger brothers and sisters after their emotionally disturbed mother abandons them. So far, Voigt has written seven books about the Tillermans.

Voigt is constantly jotting down story ideas and lists of characters.

IN ADDITION TO WORKING IN ADVERTISING AND AS A TEACHER, VOIGT HAS BEEN A CHILD-CARE PROVIDER, A SECRETARY, AND A WAITRESS.

Sometimes her ideas bounce around in her mind for more than a year before she starts turning them into a book.

In her leisure time, Voigt enjoys reading, playing tennis, seeing movies, and spending time at the beach with her children. Her many fans enjoy spending their free time reading the books of Cynthia Voigt.

❧

WHERE TO FIND OUT MORE ABOUT CYNTHIA VOIGT

BOOKS

Drew, Bernard A. *The 100 Most Popular Young Adult Authors: Biographical Sketches and Bibliographies.* Englewood, Colo.: Libraries Unlimited, 1996.

Jordan, Shirley Marie, ed. *Broken Silences: Interviews with Black and White Women Writers.* Piscataway, N.J.: Rutgers University Press, 1993.

Kovacs, Deborah, and James Preller. *Meet the Authors and Illustrators: 60 Creators of Favorite Children's Books Talk about Their Work.* Vol. 2. New York: Scholastic, 1993.

WEB SITES

BOOK REPORTER
http://www.bookreporter.com/brc/author.asp?author=2751
For information about Voigt's life and work

CYNTHIA VOIGT
http://gyabooks.tripod.com/voigt.html
To read short synopses of Voigt's books

EDUCATIONAL PAPERBACK ASSOCIATION
http://www.edupaperback.org/pastbios/Voigtcy.html
For biographical information about Voigt

———

CYNTHIA VOIGT WON THE NEWBERY MEDAL FOR *DICEY'S SONG,* THE CALIFORNIA YOUNG READER'S AWARD FOR *IZZY, WILLY-NILLY,* AND THE EDGAR ALLAN POE AWARD FOR *THE CALLENDER PAPERS.*

Bernard Waber

Born: September 27, 1924

Bernard Waber discovered his love for children's books after his own children were born. He loved to read books to them. They often wondered why he was always reading children's books instead of books for adults. One day, he decided that he could write and illustrate books for children. Since then, Waber has created more than thirty books for children. His best-known books include *Lyle, Lyle Crocodile; The House on East 88th Street; Nobody Is Perfick;* and *Ira Sleeps Over.*

Waber was born on September 27, 1924, in Philadelphia, Pennsylvania. He grew up during the Great Depression, and his family did not have much money. Bernard and his family moved many times so his

---

LYLE, LYLE, CROCODILE HAS BEEN MADE INTO A MUSICAL PLAY
AND AN ANIMATED TELEVISION SPECIAL.

father could find work. Each
time his family moved, Bernard
hoped there would be a library
and a movie theater near their
new house.

"Like food and drink, I considered the library and movies life-giving staples, and could not conceive of survival without them. The library, with its great store of un-required reading, was a banquet to which I brought a ravenous appetite."

Bernard loved books and
reading. He went to the library
as often as he could. He also
loved going to the movies. He spent almost every Saturday at the movie
theater. When he was eight years old, he got a job as an usher at a movie
theater. This job enabled him to watch the last ten or fifteen minutes of
each movie, and he used his imagination to make up stories for the
beginning and the middle of the movie.

Bernard was the youngest child in his family, and he often copied
what his older brother was doing. "The youngest of four children, I was
accustomed to all manner of hand-me-downs from an older brother,"
Waber remembers. "Luckily, my brother also handed down his great
interest in drawing." Bernard spent hours drawing pictures that he saw in
magazines.

In 1942, Waber joined the army. After that, he decided to study
painting and drawing. He enrolled in an art school in Philadelphia.

SINCE WABER CREATED LYLE THE CROCODILE IN HIS BOOKS, HE HAS FOUND
MANY DIFFERENT CROCODILE DECORATIONS FOR HIS HOME.

Lyle, Lyle, Crocodile
by BERNARD WABER

**A Selected Bibliography
of Waber's Work**

The Mouse That Snored (2000)

Gina (1995)

Nobody Is Perfick (1991)

Ira Says Goodbye (1988)

Bernard (1982)

Dear Hildegarde (1980)

Ira Sleeps Over (1972)

A Firefly Named Torchy (1970)

An Anteater Named Arthur (1967)

Lyle, Lyle, Crocodile (1965)

Just Like Abraham Lincoln (1964)

The House on East 88th Street (1962)

Waber married Ethel Bernstein in 1952 and moved to New York City. He worked as an illustrator and designer for a magazine publishing company. He loved this job because he got to work with many other talented artists. He went on to work for several magazines during his career.

In addition to his magazine work, Waber became interested

"Strangely, writing seems to come easier for me while I am in transit. I commute daily to Manhattan. As the train rattles onward, the rhythm of the wheels and the rocking motion somehow give my thoughts a fresh release."

in creating a children's book. His friends and coworkers encouraged him. His first book, *Lorenzo,* was published in 1961. His books have won many awards and remain popular with children.

Bernard Waber continues to write and illustrate children's books. He also visits schools and libraries to talk about his books. He lives in Baldwin Harbor, New York.

&

WHERE TO FIND OUT MORE ABOUT BERNARD WABER

BOOKS

Kovacs, Deborah, and James Preller. *Meet the Authors and Illustrators: 60 Creators of Favorite Children's Books Talk about Their Work.* Vol. 1. New York: Scholastic, 1991.

Silvey, Anita, ed. *Children's Books and Their Creators.* Boston: Houghton Mifflin, 1995.

WEB SITES

IRA SAYS GOODBYE

http://www.carolhurst.com/titles/irasaysgoodbye.html
For a review and relevant information about Bernard Waber's book

WABER'S BOOKS

http://hallkidstales.com/W/5.shtml
For a list of Bernard Waber's most popular books with links to further information

———

WHEN HE WAS STARTING OUT AS AN ILLUSTRATOR, WABER WORKED AT THE DINING-ROOM TABLE IN HIS SMALL APARTMENT. HE MOVED TO A SEPARATE STUDIO LATER IN HIS CAREER.

Martin Waddell

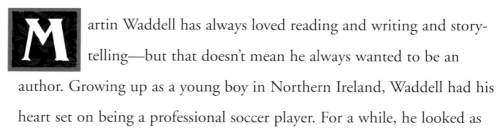

Born: April 10, 1941

Martin Waddell has always loved reading and writing and story-telling—but that doesn't mean he always wanted to be an author. Growing up as a young boy in Northern Ireland, Waddell had his heart set on being a professional soccer player. For a while, he looked as if he would succeed!

Martin Waddell was born on April 10, 1941, in Belfast, Northern Ireland. This was in the middle of World War II (1939–1945), and German bombs were falling the night he was born. To keep their new baby safe, Martin's parents moved to the country town of Newcastle, in County Down, where his family had lived for almost 400 years. The Waddells moved back to Belfast after the war but always returned to Newcastle for holidays and summer vacations.

MARTIN WADDELL USUALLY SPENDS SEVERAL WEEKS EACH YEAR GIVING WRITING WORKSHOPS IN SCHOOLS IN NORTHERN IRELAND.

When his parents divorced when he was eleven, Martin and his mother moved back to Newcastle for good.

Martin wasn't particularly fond of school. He quit when he was just fifteen. He took a short-lived job at a newspaper and then moved to London when he was sixteen, hoping to win a place on a professional soccer team. Although Martin had been a fine goalie on his Newcastle team, he soon discovered that he didn't quite have

> *"My job as a writer is not to tell children what to think or do about a given situation, but to encourage them to think for themselves."*

CAN'T YOU SLEEP, LITTLE BEAR?

Martin Waddell *illustrated by* **Barbara Firth**

A Selected Bibliography of Waddell's Work
Snow Bears (2002)
A Kitten Called Moonlight (2001)
Good Job, Little Bear! (1999)
What Use Is a Moose? (1996)
You and Me, Little Bear (1996)
The Big Big Sea (1994)
The Happy Hedgehog Band (1992)
Little Dracula at the Seashore (1992)
Owl Babies (1992)
The Pig in the Pond (1992)
The Toymaker: A Story in Two Parts (1992)
Farmer Duck (1991)
Daisy's Christmas (1990)
Amy Said (1989)
Once There Were Giants (1989)
Alice, the Artist (1988)
Can't You Sleep, Little Bear? (1988)
Harriet and the Robot (1987)
Harriet and the Haunted School (1984)
Going West (1983)
Harriet and the Crocodiles (1982)
In a Blue Velvet Dress (1972)

what it took to be a professional athlete. That's when he turned to writing as a career. After several years—and a whole stack of rejected novels—he finally made a name for himself as a successful author of comic spy thrillers for adults.

Waddell earned enough money from his books to move back to Ireland, get married, and buy a house. But it wasn't until he published his first book for children in 1972, *In a Blue Velvet Dress,* that Waddell finally found his voice. He remembers, "My lyrical novels weren't even publishable. The thrillers were hopelessly padded to make the length, but *Blue Velvet* was full of fun and adventure and emotion. I had got it right, at last!"

> *"I was lucky. I grew up with books, so the transition from being a reader to being a writer was always possible. When I write books for the very small, I have this period in mind."*

He never looked back. Waddell has been writing steadily for almost forty years. By his own count, he's finished about 180 books!

Waddlell has written children's books of all genres—mysteries and picture books, comedies and ghost stories, books about soccer players and baby bears and farmer ducks and accident-prone children. Many of his books, especially those written for very young children, were inspired by his own three sons, who are now grown up and living on their own.

———

IN 1972, WADDELL WAS NEARLY KILLED BY A TERRORIST BOMB IN A LOCAL CHURCH. HE WAS SO AFFECTED BY THE EVENT THAT HE WAS UNABLE TO WRITE FOR THE NEXT SIX YEARS.

Waddell takes even his most lighthearted books seriously, feeling that books for children need to be "quick, clear, emotionally strong, and verbally bright." He has won many awards, and his work has been made into radio and television programs. He and his wife still live in Newcastle, Northern Ireland—his first home, and his best home.

❧

WHERE TO FIND OUT MORE ABOUT MARTIN WADDELL

BOOKS

Holtze, Sally Holmes, ed. *Seventh Book of Junior Authors & Illustrators.*
New York: H. W. Wilson Company, 1996.

Pendergast, Sara, and Tom Pendergast, eds.
St. James Guide to Children's Writers.
5th ed. Detroit: St. James Press, 1999.

WEB SITES

THE ALAN REVIEW
http://scholar.lib.vt.edu/ejournals/ALAN/spring99/waddell.html
To read a message from Martin Waddell

GINN LITERACY
http://www.ginn.co.uk/literacy/aboard/waddell.asp
For a profile of Martin Waddell

O'BRIEN PRESS
http://www.obrien.ie/author.cfm?authorID=61
For a short biography and information about
many of Waddell's books

WHEN WADDELL FIRST STARTED WRITING BOOKS FOR CHILDREN, HE USED THE NAME CATHERINE SEFTON, SO YOUNG READERS WOULDN'T CONFUSE HIM WITH THE MARTIN WADDELL WHO WROTE COMEDIES AND THRILLERS FOR ADULTS.

Gertrude Chandler Warner

Born: April 16, 1890
Died: August 30, 1979

As a young girl, Gertrude Chandler Warner lived near a railroad station. Her memories of watching the train cars were an important part of her writing as a children's author. Warner is best known as the creator and writer of many of the books in the Boxcar Children series. Along with the nineteen Boxcar Children books, Warner also wrote fifteen other books for adults and children.

Gertrude Chandler Warner was born on April 16, 1890, in Putnam, Connecticut. She lived in Putnam her entire life. Gertrude was

THE AMERICAN RED CROSS HONORED GERTRUDE CHANDLER WARNER FOR
HER FIFTY YEARS OF SERVICE AS A VOLUNTEER WITH THE ORGANIZATION.

often sick as a child, so she spent much of her time reading books and writing stories.

Her sister, Frances, shared her love of reading and writing. Their mother gave the girls notebooks so they could write their stories. Both girls also kept daily journals when they were growing up.

> *"As children, we received from our mother a ten-cent blank book to prevent the house from being littered with scraps of paper containing a 'good word' or a full sentence, or even a whole article."*

When Gertrude was nine years old, she wrote and illustrated her first book. The title of the book was "Golliwogg at the Zoo." She gave it to her grandfather as a Christmas present. Every year, Gertrude and her sister gave her grandparents a book they had created.

Because of her poor health, Gertrude was not able to finish high school. She and her sister wrote stories and essays that were published in local magazines. Her first published book, *The House of Delight,* came out in 1916. The book was about her experiences as a young girl playing with her dollhouse. In 1917, she went to work for the Red Cross as a writer and to help with publicity.

Warner was about twenty-eight years old when World War I (1914–1918) ended. It was a time when schools had a difficult time finding teachers. Even though she had not finished high school or

AS AN ADULT, WARNER USED THE SAME KIND OF NOTEBOOKS FOR HER RESEARCH AND NOTES THAT SHE HAD USED WHEN SHE WAS A YOUNG GIRL.

A Selected Bibliography of Warner's Work

Mystery behind the Wall (1973)

Mystery in the Sand (1971)

Bicycle Mystery (1970)

Snowbound Mystery (1968)

Houseboat Mystery (1967)

Caboose Mystery (1966)

Schoolhouse Mystery (1965)

The Lighthouse Mystery (1963)

The Woodshed Mystery (1962)

Blue Bay Mystery (1961)

Mystery Ranch (1958)

The Yellow House Mystery (1953)

Surprise Island (1949)

The Boxcar Children, Revised Edition (1942)

The Boxcar Children (1924)

The House of Delight (1916)

attended college, Warner was hired as a teacher. She taught first grade in Putnam for more than thirty years, retiring from teaching when she was sixty years old.

The first Boxcar Children book was published in 1924. Eighteen years later, Warner revised the book so it would be easier for children who struggled to read. She wanted to make her stories interesting to encourage children who had trouble reading.

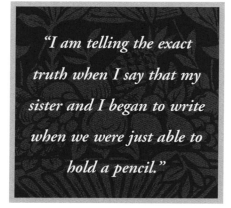

"I am telling the exact truth when I say that my sister and I began to write when we were just able to hold a pencil."

Over the years, Warner continued to write books for the Boxcar Children series. She also wrote articles and essays for magazines and newspapers.

Gertrude Chandler Warner died on August 30, 1979, at the age of eighty-nine. Since her death, other authors have continued to write books for the Boxcar Children series, which now boasts more than seventy titles.

❧

WHERE TO FIND OUT MORE ABOUT GERTRUDE CHANDLER WARNER

BOOKS

Ellsworth, Mary Ellen. *Gertrude Chandler Warner and the Boxcar Children.*
Morton Grove, Ill.: Whitman, 1997.

Wallner, Joan, and Jill Wheeler. *Gertrude Chandler Warner.*
Edina, Minn.: Abdo & Daughters, 1996.

WEB SITES

GERTRUDE CHANDLER WARNER AND THE BOXCAR CHILDREN
http://hallkidsfiction.com/people_places/222.shtml
For reviews and synopses of Warner's work

GRADE 3 BOOK REVIEWS
http://www.crockerfarm.org/meet/reviews3/Contents.htm
To read reviews of Warner's books written by children

―――

SEVERAL YEARS AGO, *THE BOXCAR CHILDREN COOKBOOK* WAS PUBLISHED. THE RECIPES WERE INSPIRED BY THE SERIES AND INCLUDE SECRET CODE BUNS, HOBO STEW, AND TREE HOUSE CHOCOLATE PUDDING.

Rosemary Wells

Born: January 29, 1943

Rosemary Wells can't remember a time when she wasn't drawing. She developed her talent at a young age. Today, she still enjoys a rewarding career as a children's writer and illustrator.

Rosemary Wells was born in New York City on January 29, 1943. Her mother was a dancer with the Russian ballet, and her father was a

playwright and actor. Rosemary grew up on the New Jersey shore, and she loved roaming around outdoors as a child. But she loved drawing even more. From the time Rosemary was two years old, her parents encouraged their artistic daughter.

After high school, Rosemary Wells studied art at the Museum School in Boston. But she and the school weren't a good match. When one of her professors told her she was "nothing

---

WELLS'S BOOK *READ TO YOUR BUNNY* INSPIRED A NATIONAL CAMPAIGN
TO PROMOTE READING ALOUD TO CHILDREN FROM AN EARLY AGE.

but an illustrator," she decided she had had enough. She left school, married Tom Wells, and went to work designing children's books.

It wasn't long before Wells stopped designing other people's books and started writing and illustrating her own. She found she had a special talent for creating books for very young readers. These books were simple and short—but they were rich with humor, feeling, and wonderful characters. Noisy

"Writing for children is as difficult as writing serious verse. Writing for children is as mysterious as writing fine music. It is as personal as singing."

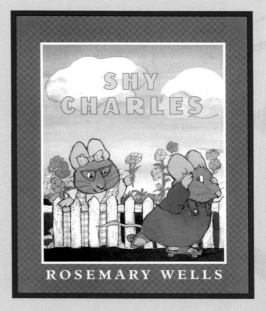

A Selected Bibliography of Wells's Work

The Secret Birthday (Text only, 2002)
Be My Valentine (Text only, 2001)
Bunny Party (2001)
Emily's First 100 Days of School (2000)
Bunny Cakes (1999)
Here Comes Mother Goose (Illustrations only, 1999)
Read to Your Bunny (1998)
First Tomato (1992)
Max's Dragon Shirt (1991)
Max's Chocolate Chicken (1989)
Shy Charles (1988)
Through the Hidden Door (1987)
Hazel's Amazing Mother (1985)
Timothy Goes to School (1981)
When No One Was Looking (1980)
Stanley & Rhoda (1978)
Benjamin & Tulip (1973)
Noisy Nora (1973)

Wells's Major Literary Awards

1989 *Boston Globe–Horn Book* Picture Book Award
 Shy Charles

> *"Emotion and humor are what make a children's book right. And it's what makes it original, and it's what makes it want to be read again and again. Children's books must be written—published to be read a hundred or two hundred times. The story comes first, the pictures come second."*

Nora, Shy Charles, Stanley and Rhoda, Max and Ruby, Hazel, Benjamin, and Tulip, Timothy, and Morris—the list of beloved Rosemary Wells characters just goes on and on.

Much of Wells's inspiration has come from her home life. Her West Highland white terriers, have been models for many of her animal characters. And her daughters inspired the Max books and many others. In fact, one reason Wells started making books for very young readers was that she couldn't find anything funny and right to read to her own daughters when they were young. "I wanted to give children adventures they could understand and include jokes parents would recognize," she explains.

Besides writing and illustrating picture and board books, Wells has written novels for middle-schoolers and teenagers. She has also illustrated two huge collections of Mother Goose rhymes. For these, she worked with Iona Opie, a British expert on folk tales and nursery rhymes. Wells loved working on the Mother Goose collections. She says, "Mother Goose herself brought me to a level, spiritually, as an illustrator, that I

PEOPLE OFTEN ASK WELLS WHERE SHE GETS HER IDEAS. SHE ANSWERS, "REALLY WHAT WE DO AS ARTISTS IS FIND. THE IDEAS COME FROM THE CLOUDS, THEY PRE-EXIST."

never knew I could achieve, and now I can't go down from there."

Rosemary Wells has written and illustrated more than sixty books during her thirty-year career. She has won many awards and has millions of fans. She shows no sign of slowing down. Wells explains, "The job I have now—writing and illustrating children's books—is pure delight. There are hard parts, but no bad or boring parts, and that is more than can be said for any other line of work I know."

⚬

WHERE TO FIND OUT MORE ABOUT ROSEMARY WELLS

BOOKS

Kovacs, Deborah, and James Preller. *Meet the Authors and Illustrators: 60 Creators of Favorite Children's Books Talk about Their Work.* Vol. 2. New York: Scholastic, 1993.

Something about the Author. Autobiography Series. Vol. 1. Detroit: Gale Research, 1986.

WEB SITES

HORN BOOKS
http://www.hbook.com/exhibit/wellsradio.html
To read an interview with Rosemary Wells

HOUGHTON MIFFLIN
http://www.eduplace.com/kids/hmr/mtai/wells.html
To read about author and illustrator Rosemary Wells

THE WORLD OF ROSEMARY WELLS
http://www.rosemarywells.com/
To visit Rosemary Wells's own Web site

——

WELLS SAYS THAT MANY OF HER BOOKS COME FROM EVERYDAY EVENTS. SHE ADMITS, "AUTHORS ARE ACCOMPLISHED EAVESDROPPERS, AND HAVE WONDERFUL SELECTIVE MEMORY."

E. B. White

Born: July 11, 1899
Died: October 1, 1985

 B. White wrote only three books for children—but they include the classics *Stuart Little* and *Charlotte's Web.* White also had a long career as a magazine writer and editor.

Elwyn Brooks (E. B.) White was born on July 11, 1899, in Mount

Vernon, New York. His father owned a company that manufactured pianos. As a boy, Elwyn was always busy writing. In fact, he began writing as soon as he knew how to spell. "I was no good at drawing, so I used words instead," White once explained. "As I grew older, I found that writing could be a way of earning a living."

IN 1963, WHITE WAS ONE OF THIRTY-ONE AMERICANS TO RECEIVE THE PRESIDENTIAL MEDAL FOR FREEDOM FROM PRESIDENT JOHN F. KENNEDY.

After finishing high school, White attended Cornell University in Ithaca, New York. He served as the editor of the college newspaper.

After he graduated from Cornell in 1921, he worked as a reporter in New York for about a year. Then he and a friend drove across the country. He found a job

"I had no intention of writing a book for children, however, and the thing merely grew, by slow stages, over a period of about twelve years. Storytelling does not come easily or naturally to me; I am more of a commentator than a spinner of yarns."

as a reporter in Seattle, Washington. He worked there for a year before returning to New York City. There, he was hired as a writer for *The New Yorker* magazine, where he remained for the next fifty years, writing poems, essays, and stories. His essays and stories also appeared in several other magazines.

In 1939, White had an idea for a children's book, and he told parts of the story to his nieces and nephews. In 1945, he finished writing his story about the little mouse named Stuart Little.

White and his wife, a *New Yorker* editor, owned a small farm in Maine. He kept animals on his farm and enjoyed spending time in the barn. While watching the animals in the barn, White came up with the idea for another book. "One day when I was on my way to feed the pig,

NO ONE KNEW WHITE WAS WORKING ON *CHARLOTTE'S WEB*. HIS PUBLISHER WAS SURPRISED WHEN SHE RECEIVED THE MANUSCRIPT.

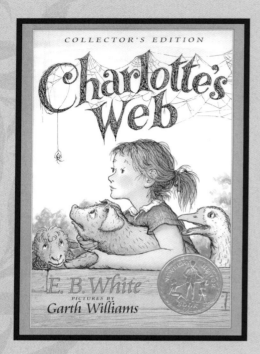

A Selected Bibliography
of White's Work

The Trumpet of the Swan (1970)

Charlotte's Web (1952)

Stuart Little (1945)

White's Major Literary Awards

1970 Laura Ingalls Wilder Award

1953 Newbery Honor Book
 Charlotte's Web

I began feeling sorry for the pig because, like most pigs, he was doomed to die," White remembered. "This made me sad. So I started thinking of ways to save a pig's life." Thinking about the pig inspired him to write *Charlotte's Web,* which was published in 1952.

White did not publish his third book for children until

"Children are a wonderful audience—they are so eager, so receptive, so quick. I have great respect for their powers of observation and reasoning. But like any good writer, I write to amuse myself, not some imaginary audience."

1970. He decided to write *The Trumpet of the Swan* because of his love of the trumpeter swans he saw at the zoo. The book tells the story of Louis, a swan without a voice.

E. B. White died on October 1, 1985. He was eighty-six years old.

❧

WHERE TO FIND OUT MORE ABOUT E. B. WHITE

BOOKS

Agosta, Lucien L. *E. B. White: The Children's Books.*
New York: Twayne Publishing, 1995.

Faber, Doris. *Great Lives: American Literature.* New York:
Atheneum Books for Young Readers, 1995.

Gherman, Beverly. *E. B. White: Some Writer!*
New York: Atheneum Publications, 1992.

Tingum, Janice. *E. B. White: The Elements of a Writer.*
Minneapolis: Lerner, 1995.

WEB SITES

EDUCATIONAL PAPERBACK ASSOCIATION
http://www.edupaperback.org/authorbios/White_EB.html
For an autobiographical sketch by White

HARPERCHILDRENS
http://www.harperchildrens.com/catalog/author_xml.asp?authorID=10499
For a biography of E. B. White and an outline of his work

HOUGHTON MIFFLIN READING
http://www.eduplace.com/kids/hmr/mtai/white.html
To read a short biography of E. B. White

———

WHITE IS THE COAUTHOR OF *THE ELEMENTS OF STYLE*. THIS
BOOK ABOUT WRITING IS USED IN MANY HIGH SCHOOL AND COLLEGE
ENGLISH AND JOURNALISM CLASSES.

David Wiesner

Born: February 5, 1956

When readers enter the wild and wonderful world of a David Wiesner book, they never know where they'll end up. Wiesner writes and illustrates children's picture books, and he loves to create books that tell stories without words. He likes readers to use their own imagination as they travel through his books. Over the years, Wiesner's unique style and interesting way of looking at the world have earned him many awards and honors.

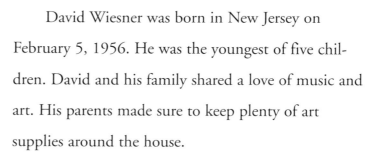

David Wiesner was born in New Jersey on February 5, 1956. He was the youngest of five children. David and his family shared a love of music and art. His parents made sure to keep plenty of art supplies around the house.

Some of David's earliest artistic influences included Bugs Bunny cartoons, *MAD* magazine, and comic books. Later, David read about great artists at his local

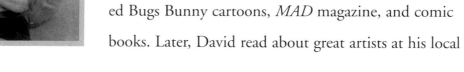

WHEN WIESNER WAS A CHILD, HIS FAVORITE THING TO DRAW WAS DINOSAURS.

library. He was especially fascinated by artists called surrealists.
These artists drew pictures of
strange and bizarre things.

Wiesner began his career as
an artist while he was still a
student at the Rhode Island
School of Design. His first
paying job was creating a cover
illustration for *Cricket,* a children's magazine. Ten years later,
Wiesner was asked to create
another cover for *Cricket.* This
time, he was allowed to draw
whatever he liked, and he
decided to draw frogs. Later,

> *"A wordless book is a very*
> *personal experience for the*
> *reader. Each person reads*
> *the book differently."*

DAVID WIESNER

A Selected Bibliography of Wiesner's Work

The Three Pigs (2001)
Sector 7 (1999)
Night of the Gargoyles (Illustrations only, 1994)
Tongues of Jade (Illustrations only, 1991)
Tuesday (1991)
Hurricane (1990)
The Rainbow People (Illustrations only, 1989)
Firebrat (Illustrations only, 1988)
Free Fall (1988)
The Loathsome Dragon (1987)
The Wand: The Return to Mesmeria (Illustrations only, 1985)
Neptune Rising: Songs and Tales of the Undersea Folk
(Illustrations only, 1982)
Owly (Illustrations only, 1982)
The Boy Who Spoke Chimp (Illustrations only, 1981)
The One Bad Thing about Birthdays (Illustrations only, 1981)
The Ugly Princess (Illustrations only, 1981)
Honest Andrew (Illustrations only, 1980)
Man from the Sky (Illustrations only, 1980)

Wiesner's Major Literary Awards

2002 Caldecott Medal
  The Three Pigs

2000 Caldecott Honor Book
  Sector 7

1992 Caldecott Medal
  Tuesday

1989 Caldecott Honor Book
  Free Fall

> "*Growing up in New Jersey, my friends and I re-created our world daily. The neighborhood would become anything from the far reaches of the universe to a prehistoric jungle. To believe that giant pterodactyls were swooping down on us required only a small leap of faith.*"

he created an entire book about frogs, called *Tuesday.*

At first, Wiesner illustrated the works of other authors. He has illustrated the works of Avi, Eve Bunting, Jane Yolen, and many others. Beginning in 1987, however, Wiesner began coming up with his own story ideas and illustrating them. One of his first solo projects was *The Loathsome Dragon.* Wiesner and his wife, Kim Kahng, worked on the book together. His next solo project, *Free Fall,* was completely without words.

Many people ask Wiesner where he gets the ideas for his stories. Some ideas come from events in his own life. Wiesner got the idea for *Hurricane,* for example, from a big storm that happened when he was a kid. Lots of Wiesner's ideas come straight from his very active imagination. For instance, he got ideas for *Tuesday* by asking himself, "If I were a frog and I discovered I could fly, where would I go? What would I do?" Wiesner is especially fascinated by flying. Frogs, fish, and even vegetables have flown through his stories!

Wiesner's fantastic imagination and vivid watercolor drawings

———

IN HIGH SCHOOL, DAVID WIESNER CREATED WORDLESS COMIC BOOKS. ONE OF HIS FIRST WAS CALLED "SLOP THE WONDER PIG." LATER, HE AND HIS FRIENDS MADE A SILENT MOVIE ABOUT VAMPIRES.

have earned him a reputation as one of the best children's illustrators today. They have also earned him many awards and honors. Wiesner is a two-time winner of the Caldecott Medal.

In 1997, David Wiesner dove into something new. He created the illustrations for a CD-ROM game called *The Day the World Broke.* The game features flying cows, underground elevators, and talking machines. It was a big hit. No matter what Wiesner draws, his energy and imagination make his work fun for people of all ages.

❧

WHERE TO FIND OUT MORE ABOUT DAVID WIESNER

BOOKS
Holtze, Sally Holmes, ed. *Seventh Book of Junior Authors & Illustrators.*
New York: H. W. Wilson Company, 1996.

WEB SITES
NATIONAL CENTER FOR CHILDREN'S
ILLUSTRATED LITERATURE
http://www.nccil.org/children/wiesner01.html
For samples of Wiesner's work, with synopses of some of his books

---

WHEN DAVID WIESNER WAS IN FOURTH GRADE, HIS TEACHER SENT
AN ANGRY NOTE HOME TO HIS PARENTS. THE NOTE SAID, "DAVID WOULD
RATHER BE DRAWING THAN DOING HIS WORK."

Laura Ingalls Wilder

Born: February 7, 1867
Died: February 10, 1957

Most people think of the author Laura Ingalls Wilder as the child in the Little House books. But the person that wrote the books was not a child. Laura Ingalls Wilder didn't publish *Little House in the Big Woods* until she was sixty-five years old! Before that time, she wrote some articles for local newspapers and major magazines. Her daughter, Rose, a professional writer in California, really got her writing seriously. Rose encouraged her mother to write the stories of

---

IN 1954, THE LAURA INGALLS WILDER AWARD WAS CREATED. GIVEN ONCE EVERY TWO YEARS, IT HONORS AN AUTHOR WHO HAS PUBLISHED SEVERAL WORKS IMPORTANT TO THE LIVES OF CHILDREN.

her childhood experiences. Wilder wrote the books to entertain children and to preserve the stories of what pioneer life on the prairie was like when she was a child. She made sure that each book she wrote was told through the eyes and with the voice of a child.

Laura Ingalls Wilder was born on Febrary 7, 1867 in Pepin, Wisconsin. Her parents, Caroline and Charles Ingalls, had four daughters. Laura was the second oldest. Charles Ingalls thought of himself as a pioneer. Like her father, Laura enjoyed moving. She always felt that home was not where a house was, or where she decided to live, but where her family was.

"It is still best to be honest and truthful; to make the most of what we have; to be happy with simple pleasures and to be cheerful and have courage when things go wrong."

"Every American has always been free to pursue his happiness, and so long as Americans are free they will continue to make our country even more wonderful."

The eight books in the Little House series tell the story of her life from when she was a five-year-old living in the Wisconsin woods through her early adult years in De Smet, South Dakota. The books share the experiences of the Ingalls family as Laura's father led them farther into the frontier.

Because they moved many times, Laura went to many schools. Although she never graduated

WILDER DIDN'T HAVE TIME TO WRITE REPLIES TO EVERY PERSON WHO WROTE HER A LETTER. INSTEAD, SHE CAME UP WITH ONE LETTER THAT ANSWERED THE QUESTIONS THAT MOST PEOPLE ASKED HER.

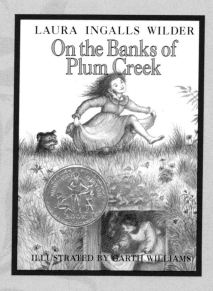

A Selected Bibliography of Wilder's Work

The First Four Years (1971)

These Happy Golden Years (1943)

Little Town on the Prairie (1941)

The Long Winter (1940)

By the Shores of Silver Lake (1939)

On the Banks of Plum Creek (1937)

Little House on the Prairie (1935)

Farmer Boy (1933)

Little House in the Big Woods (1932)

Wilder's Major Literary Awards

1954 Laura Ingalls Wilder Award

1944 Newbery Honor Book
  These Happy Golden Years

1942 Newbery Honor Book
  Little Town on the Prairie

1941 Newbery Honor Book
  The Long Winter

1940 Newbery Honor Book
  By the Shores of Silver Lake

1938 Newbery Honor Book
  On the Banks of Plum Creek

from high school, she did earn a teaching certificate in 1882. She took a job in a school several miles from her parents' home. Almost three years later, on August 25, 1885, she married Almanzo Wilder. Laura Ingalls Wilder included their life together in her Little House stories.

Wilder lived in her Mansfield, Missouri, home until February 10, 1957, when she died of a stroke. She received letters from fans around the world right up until the time she died.

It has been more than seventy years since Wilder published *Little House in the Big Woods.* And more than one hundred years have passed since the stories actually took place. But children today continue to read and love the stories of Laura, Mary, Carrie, baby Grace, Ma, and Pa living in the wilderness, experiencing a life that can only be imagined through the words of Laura Ingalls Wilder.

ॐ

WHERE TO FIND OUT MORE ABOUT LAURA INGALLS WILDER

BOOKS

Anderson, William. *Laura Ingalls Wilder: A Biography.* New York: HarperCollins, 1992.

Giff, Patricia Reilly. *Laura Ingalls Wilder: Growing Up in the Little House.*
New York: Viking Kestrel, 1987.

Greene, Carol. *Laura Ingalls Wilder: Author of the Little House Books.*
Chicago: Children's Press, 1990.

Wadsworth, Ginger. *Laura Ingalls Wilder: A Storyteller of the Prairie.*
Minneapolis: Lerner, 1996.

WEB SITES

LAURA INGALLS WILDER HOME AND MUSEUM
http://www.lauraingallswilderhome.com/
To read an open letter from Wilder, view pictures of Wilder and her family, and download a map of Wilder's travels

---

IN THE 1970S AND 1980S, A TELEVISION SERIES TITLED *LITTLE HOUSE ON THE PRAIRIE,* BASED ON WILDER'S STORIES, WAS VERY POPULAR. IT STARRED MICHAEL LANDON AS CHARLES INGALLS AND MELISSA GILBERT AS LAURA.

Garth Williams

Born: April 16, 1912
Died: May 8, 1996

Charlotte, a kindhearted spider; Chester Cricket; and Stuart Little are but a few of the famous storybook characters Garth Williams illustrated with pen and ink. Generations of children have fallen in love with the gentle characters he brought to life for some of the most distinguished children's authors of his time—Margaret Wise Brown, George Selden, E. B. White, and Laura Ingalls Wilder. Although Williams wrote

seven children's books of his own, he is better known as an illustrator than as an author.

Garth Montgomery Williams was born in New York City on April 16, 1912. Both of his parents were artists. Garth's father, a cartoonist, drew for *Punch*, a British magazine. His mother was a landscape painter.

WILLIAMS SPENT SEVERAL YEARS ILLUSTRATING LAURA INGALLS WILDER'S
LITTLE HOUSE BOOKS. HE CALLED IT "A MOST EXCITING ADVENTURE."

Garth lived on a farm in New Jersey until the age of ten, when his family moved to England.

In England, Garth Williams studied painting, design, and sculpture at the Westminster Art School and the Royal Academy of Art. When he finished his studies, Williams became headmaster of the Luton Art School outside of London.

"*Everybody in my home was always either painting or drawing. . . . [I grew up as] a typical Huckleberry Finn, roaming barefoot around the farm, watching the farmer milk his cows by hand.*"

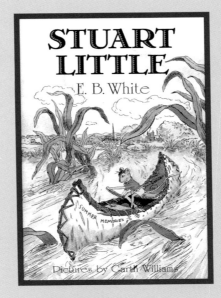

A Selected Bibliography of Williams's Work

Beneath a Blue Umbrella (Illustrations only, 1990)
Over and Over (Illustrations only, 1987)
Self-Portrait: Garth Williams (1982)
Bedtime for Frances (Illustrations only, 1960)
The Rabbits' Wedding (1958)
Baby Farm Animals (1953)
The Little House series (Illustrations only, 1953)
My Bedtime Book (1953)
Baby Animals (1952)
Charlotte's Web (Illustrations only, 1952)
The Adventures of Benjamin Pink (1951)
Stuart Little (Illustrations only, 1945)

> *"Illustrating books is not just making pictures of the houses, the people and the articles mentioned by the author; the artist has to see everything with the same eyes."*

In his spare time, he painted murals.

In 1941, Williams returned to the United States, eager to find work. *The New Yorker* magazine hired him as a cartoonist and illustrator. While there, he illustrated E. B. White's book *Stuart Little,* which launched his career as a children's book illustrator. In this first work for children, Williams showcased his ability to create characters that looked like animals but walked and talked like humans. He kept this style in later books, giving each animal a human personality with hopes and dreams.

In 1952, Williams worked with E. B. White on another book, *Charlotte's Web,* the story of a spider who saves a pig's life. It has since become a classic in children's literature.

During the 1950s, Williams also illustrated eight of Laura Ingalls Wilder's Little House books about the American frontier. His illustrations depict what pioneer life was like for the Ingalls family, who lived in the forests of Wisconsin and on the prairies of Kansas, Minnesota, and Dakota Territory.

Williams continued illustrating children's books during the 1980s. His long, successful career came to an end on May 8, 1996, when he

GARTH WILLIAMS HAD FOUR WIVES, FIVE DAUGHTERS, AND ONE SON. HIS FIRST DAUGHTER, FIONA, WAS HIS MODEL FOR FERN, THE LITTLE GIRL IN THE BOOK *CHARLOTTE'S WEB.*

died of cancer at his home in Guanajuato, Mexico.

Always a respectful illustrator, Garth Williams worked well with authors. He had discovered early in his career how to see events and characters through an author's eyes. This gift enabled him to please his authors and fascinate his readers. For more than fifty years, his warm-hearted characters have delighted children of all ages.

❧

WHERE TO FIND OUT MORE ABOUT GARTH WILLIAMS

BOOKS

Something about the Author. Autobiography Series.
Vol. 7. Detroit: Gale Research, 1989.

Williams, Garth. *Self-Portrait: Garth Williams.*
Boston: Addison Wesley Longman, 1982.

WEB SITES

BIOGRAPHY
http://webpages.marshall.edu/~irby1/laura/garth.html
To read a biography of Garth

THE DEFINITIVE LAURA INGALLS WILDER PAGES:
A BIOGRAPHY OF GARTH WILLIAMS
http://vvv.com/~jenslegg/williams.htm
For information about Williams's life and work

———

MOST OF WILLIAMS'S ILLUSTRATIONS FOR GRADE-SCHOOL CHILDREN WERE DONE IN BLACK AND WHITE. AT THE TIME, PUBLISHING BOOKS IN COLOR WAS VERY COSTLY.

David Wisniewski

Born: March 21, 1953
Died: September 12, 2002

Some people seem to be born knowing they want to be authors. Others make discoveries along the way that lead them to that career. It would be hard to find a better example of that process of discovery than David Wisniewski, who became an author and illustrator by first being a clown and a puppeteer.

David Wisniewski was born on March 21, 1953. His father was in the U.S. military, and the family lived in England, Nebraska, Texas, and Germany while David was growing up. Wisniewski wanted to study theater but he ran out of money after one semester in college. He learned that the Ringling Brothers and Barnum & Bailey Circus would pay him to go to its clown college, so he signed up. He learned acrobatics and

DAVID WISNIEWSKI'S FIRST BOOK AS AN ILLUSTRATOR, *DUCKY*, IS BASED ON A NEWS STORY ABOUT A CRATE OF **29,000** RUBBER DUCKIES WASHED OVERBOARD FROM A CARGO SHIP IN A STORM.

juggling, as well as how to ride a unicycle. He then spent three years as a clown for Ringling and for Circus Vargas.

When circus life got tiring, Wisniewski took what he knew about performing and got a job at a puppet theater. His boss, Donna Harris, soon became his wife. Their specialty was shadow puppetry—in which flat figures of cut-out paper cast shadows on a screen. When they had children and wanted to stop touring, the couple started a graphic-design company.

Wisniewski met a former chil-dren's book editor who was so impressed with his work that she gave him the name of an editor and told him to visit her right away. Wisniewski didn't. He spent

"I think if you truly want to do some-thing—you can. The problem is—in art or any discipline—one gets discouraged and stops. When I pursue something difficult, I often keep in mind something former president Calvin Coolidge said: 'Everything yields to diligence.'"

months planning. When he finally went to see the editor, he had a story and several finished illustrations.

That story became his first book, *The Warrior and the Wise Man*. Set in Japan, it is the adventure of two samurai brothers—one brave, and one wise. The book has two Wisniewski trademarks.

First, the story was written to fit in with real Japanese legends.

REAL CLOWNS IN THE CIRCUS PAINT BIG RED MOUTHS ONLY ON THEIR LOWER LIPS, SAID WISNIEWSKI. YOU CAN SEE IT IN THE ILLUSTRATIONS HE DREW FOR *AMANDA JOINS THE CIRCUS*, BY AVI.

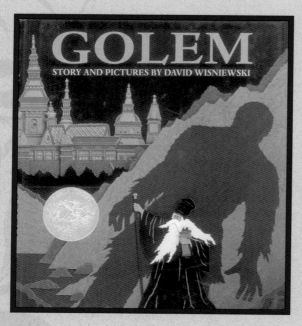

A Selected Bibliography of Wisniewski's Work

Master Man: A Tall Tale of Nigeria (Illustrations only, 2001)

The Secret Knowledge of Grown-Ups: The Second File (2001)

I'll Play with You (Illustrations only, 2000)

Amanda Joins the Circus (Illustrations only, 1999)

Keep Your Eye on Amanda (Illustrations only, 1999)

Tough Cookie (1999)

Workshop (Illustrations only, 1999)

The Secret Knowledge of Grown-Ups (1998)

Ducky (Illustrations only, 1997)

Golem (1996)

The Wave of the Sea-Wolf (1994)

Sundiata: Lion King of Mali (1992)

Rain Player (1991)

Elfwyn's Saga (1990)

The Warrior and the Wise Man (1989)

Wisniewski's Major Literary Awards

1997 Caldecott Medal
  Golem

Wisniewski carefully researched the customs and beliefs of the people he wrote about. He wrote folktales set in Africa *(Sundiata: Lion King of Mali),* ancient Iceland *(Elfwyn's Saga),* and North America's Mayan and Tlingit cultures *(Rain Player* and *The Wave of the Sea-Wolf).*

Second, *The Warrior and the Wise Man* displays Wisniewski's trademark style of art. From his days working with shadow puppets, Wisniewski was skilled in making illustrations out of cut paper. Each illustration contains up to twelve layers of paper. Wisniewski did his cutting with small knives. He wore out about 800 blades for each book.

In 1997, Wisniewski won

the Caldecott Medal for *Golem,* a dark tale about a clay giant brought to life to guard a Jewish ghetto of long-ago Prague. Until his death on September 12, 2002, Wisniewski continued to think of writing for children as a serious calling. "What a privilege!" he said. "What a responsibility!"

"I try to create richly detailed, obsessively accurate, original folktales set in ancient cultures, but with modern messages. I consider the work my ministry; my service to others."

WHERE TO FIND OUT MORE ABOUT DAVID WISNIEWSKI

BOOKS

Holtze, Sally Holmes, ed. *Seventh Book of Junior Authors & Illustrators.* New York: H. W. Wilson Company, 1996.

WEB SITES

AMERICAN LIBRARY ASSOCIATION
http://www.ala.org/alsc/wisniew.html
For information about Wisniewski's life and work

ASK THE AUTHOR
http://www.eduplace.com/rdg/author/wisniewski/question.html
To read an interview with David Wisniewski

ILLUSTRATED BOOKS BY DAVID WISNIEWSKI
http://scils.rutgers.edu/~kvander/golem/davidw.html
To see examples of Wisniewski's work

WISNIEWSKI HAD NO FORMAL ART TRAINING. HE JOKED THAT HE WENT TO "THE STAN LEE SCHOOL OF ARTISTS"—MEANING THAT HE STUDIED ART BY LOOKING AT THE DRAWINGS IN MARVEL COMICS, PUBLISHED BY STAN LEE.

Audrey Wood
Don Wood

Born: 1948 (Audrey)
Born: May 4, 1945 (Don)

Audrey and Don Wood work together on their children's books. Audrey comes up with an idea for a book. She then shares it with Don to see if he wants to illustrate it. Sometimes he does the illustrations, and other times they decide to have Audrey illustrate the book. After being married for more than three decades, they just know who should illustrate each project. The Woods have worked on many books together, including *The Napping House, King Bidgood's in the Bathtub,* and *Jubal's Wish.* Audrey has also written and illustrated many of her own books.

Audrey Wood was born in 1948 in Little Rock, Arkansas. There were many artists in her family,

---

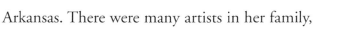

IN HIS JOB WITH THE CIRCUS, AUDREY WOOD'S FATHER PAINTED
THE MURALS FOR THE BIG TOP AND THE SIDESHOWS.

including both her father and grandfather. When she was a toddler, Audrey and her family lived in Florida. Her father worked as a painter for the Ringling Brothers and Barnum & Bailey Circus. Her family then moved to Mexico, where her parents studied art.

As a child, Audrey took lessons in dance, drama, and art.

"I would open one of my parents' lavishly illustrated art books and make up stories about the paintings. The nature encyclopedia was also one of our favorites, especially the section on reptiles and amphibians."
—Audrey Wood

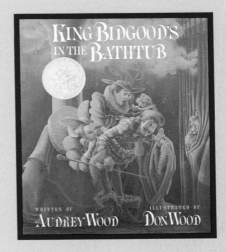

A Selected Bibliography of the Woods' Work

Jubal's Wish (2000)
Bright and Early Thursday Evening: A Tangled Tale (1996)
Silly Sally (1992)
Piggies (1991)
Oh My Baby Bear! (1990)
Weird Parents (1989)
Elbert's Bad Word (1988)
Heckedy Peg (1987)
King Bidgood's in the Bathtub (1985)
The Napping House (1984)
Moonflute (1980)

The Woods' Major Literary Awards

1986 Caldecott Honor Book
  King Bidgood's in the Bathtub

> *"A picture book is at least half theater or half film. Rhythm is an extremely important element. Also critical is point of view. . . . Maybe because we've both worked in theater . . . we're sensitive to split-second nuances that can make or break a show, or a picture book. For us, the page is a stage."*
> —Don Wood

She knew that she wanted to be an artist.

Don Wood was born on May 4, 1945, in Atwater, California. He grew up on a farm where peaches, oranges, grapes, almonds, and sweet potatoes were grown. Don worked very hard. When he was in sixth grade, he was put in charge of forty acres of the farm.

Don loved to draw, but he was too busy on the farm most of the time. "Winter was my time to draw," Wood remembers, "so I did constantly." Like his future wife, he too knew that he wanted to be an artist when he grew up.

Audrey and Don met in California in the 1960s when they were both studying art. They were married in 1969, and soon thereafter, they traveled to Mexico and Guatemala. They brought home pottery and sculpture made by Indian artists. They used it to open an art shop in Arkansas.

After their son was born, Audrey decided to make a career change. She wanted to become a children's book author. She thought that it would be best for them to move to New York City because there were

TO MAKE HIS DRAWINGS MORE REALISTIC, DON WOOD OFTEN USES HUMAN MODELS FOR HIS PICTURES. BOTH HIS WIFE AND THEIR SON, BRUCE, HAVE MODELED FOR HIM.

many publishers there. Instead, Don convinced her to move to California.

The first book that Audrey and Don Wood worked on together was *Moonflute.* Audrey wrote the story, and Don created the illustrations. Since then, they have written and illustrated more than ten books together. Audrey and Don Wood continue to create children's books. They live in Santa Barbara, California.

⌘

WHERE TO FIND OUT MORE ABOUT AUDREY AND DON WOOD

BOOKS
Holtze, Sally Holmes, ed. *Sixth Book of Junior Authors & Illustrators.* New York: H .W. Wilson Company, 1989.

Something about the Author. Vol. 50. Detroit: Gale Research, 1988.

WEB SITES
ARTIST AT A GLANCE
http://www.friend.ly.net/scoop/biographies/wooddon/
For a biography of Don Wood

THE AUDREY WOOD WEB SITE
http://www.audreywood.com/
For information on Audrey Wood's past, current, and upcoming projects

CHILDREN'S BOOK AUTHORS AND ILLUSTRATORS
http://hallkidstales.com/W/14.shtml
To learn more about books by Audrey and Don Wood

WHEN HE WAS A YOUNG BOY, DON WOOD COULD NOT FIND PAPER LARGE ENOUGH FOR HIS DRAWINGS. HE WOULD USE THE PAPER THAT THE FAMILY'S LAUNDRY CAME WRAPPED IN.

Betty Ren Wright

Born: June 15, 1927

Almost all children are thrilled by a scary story. That is one reason why author Betty Ren Wright is so popular. Wright is a children's book author, and many of her books are ghost stories and mysteries. Some of her books include *The Dollhouse Murders, Christina's Ghost,* and *The Pike River Phantom.*

Wright was born on June 15, 1927, in Wakefield, Michigan. Both her father and her mother were teachers. Betty enjoyed writing as a child.

BETTY REN WRIGHT'S SHORT STORIES HAVE BEEN PUBLISHED IN *REDBOOK, LADIES' HOME JOURNAL,* AND *COSMOPOLITAN.*

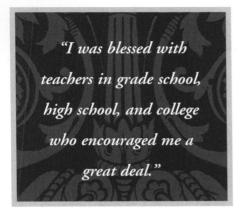

"I was blessed with teachers in grade school, high school, and college who encouraged me a great deal."

She says, "My first book was a collection of poems begun when I was seven. My mother bought a black loose-leaf notebook, had my name lettered on it, and there it was—a dream come true, a dream that I wanted to repeat."

Throughout school, teachers encouraged Betty to write, and they also gave her some advice. They told her to have another job while she was writing so that she would have a regular paycheck.

After she graduated from high school, Wright attended what is now Lawrence University of Wisconsin. She remembered the advice of her teachers. When she had earned her college degree, she got a job as an editorial assistant. She worked with authors to publish their writing.

Meanwhile, Wright wrote her own stories in her free time. Most of these stories were short fiction for adults. Finally, in 1978, she decided to quit her editing job and become a full-time writer.

Wright planned to focus on fiction for adults. But first, she

"Each of my books has sizeable chunks of my own life in it—people or events or feelings, or all three."

IN 1954, WRIGHT PUBLISHED *MR. MOGGS' DOGS* UNDER THE
NAME REVENA, WHICH IS HER MOTHER'S NAME.

A Selected Bibliography of Wright's Work

The Moonlight Man (2000)
The Wish Master (2000)
A Ghost in the Family (1998)
The Cat Next Door (1991)
The Pike River Phantom (1988)
Christina's Ghost (1985)
Ghosts beneath Our Feet (1984)
The Dollhouse Murders (1983)
The Secret Window (1982)
Good Morning, Farm (1964)
Poppyseed (1954)
Yellow Cat (1952)
Getting Rid of Marjorie (1981)
Willy Woo-oo-oo (1951)

decided to write one story for young readers. It was called *Getting Rid of Marjorie.* She enjoyed it so much that she decided to write one more for children. Then, she wrote another and another. Today, she's still writing stories for children.

"I love being scared!" Wright says. So it is not a surprise that many of her books are ghost stories and mysteries.

The ideas for Wright's stories come from events and experiences in her own life. She gets ideas from things she sees in the park, people in her life, and places she has visited. She wrote about a boy, Charlie Hocking, in *The Pike River Phantom* because someone asked her why all her books were about girls.

Betty Ren Wright gives speeches about her work and often conducts workshops. She continues to write novels and short stories for children and adults. "The best moments of all come when I hear from boys and girls who have enjoyed what I had to tell," says Wright. "Until a reader says 'I like it!' writing a book is a little like talking into an empty room." She lives in Kenosha, Wisconsin, with her husband, George Frederiksen, who is an artist.

❧

WHERE TO FIND OUT MORE ABOUT BETTY REN WRIGHT

BOOKS

Holtze, Sally Holmes, ed. *Sixth Book of Junior Authors & Illustrators.*
New York: H. W. Wilson Company, 1989.

WEB SITES

OUTLINE OF THE MOONLIGHT MAN
http://www.secondaryenglish.com/moonlightman.html
For information about Betty Ren Wright's book
The Moonlight Man

REBECCA CANDILL YOUNG READERS'
BOOK AWARD 1989 WINNER
http://www.rebeccacandill.org/PastWinners/1989/1989books.htm
For a descriptive booklist of Wright's novels

———

WRIGHT'S STORIES HAVE BEEN PUBLISHED IN DANISH, SPANISH, AND SWEDISH.

Laurence Yep

Born: June 14, 1948

Laurence Yep grew up in San Francisco, California, surrounded by three cultures—white, black, and Asian. Yet he never really felt a part of any one of them, even though he is Chinese American. When he entered high school, he felt ignored by the other students. So, in his quiet way, he fought back. He began writing works of science fiction and filled them with places and characters unlike any he had known before. In his own made-up universe, life could work out just the way Yep wanted.

Laurence Yep was born on June 14, 1948, in San Francisco. He published his first science fiction story when he was just eighteen. After graduating from college, he published his first book, *Sweetwater,* about an early colonist from planet Earth who visits a star called Harmony.

LATER GATOR WAS INSPIRED BY A REAL-LIFE REPTILE. WHEN YEP WAS YOUNGER, HE KEPT A PET ALLIGATOR NAMED OSCAR.

After this early success, Yep decided to explore his Chinese heritage. His ideas about his grandparents' homeland came from stories he had been told as a child. In this China, there was no Great Wall or Imperial Palace, only small villages filled with people who longed to go to America—the "Golden Mountain"—to work and become rich. For Yep, Chinese legends and myths mixed together with tales of real life.

> "I get the ideas from everything. Children sometimes think you have to have special experiences to write, but good writing brings out what's special in ordinary things."

A Selected Bibliography of Yep's Work

Spring Pearl: The Last Flower (2002)

Angelfish (2001)

Dream Soul (2000)

The Magic Paintbrush (2000)

The Amah (1999)

The Imp That Ate My Homework (1998)

Later Gator (1995)

Dragon's Gate (1993)

The Man Who Tricked a Ghost (1993)

Dragon Cauldron (1991)

The Lost Garden (1991)

The Star Fisher (1991)

Tongues of Jade (1991)

The Rainbow People (1989)

Dragon Steel (1985)

Dragon of the Lost Sea (1982)

Child of the Owl (1977)

Dragonwings (1975)

Sweetwater (1973)

Yep's Major Literary Awards

1994 Newbery Honor Book
  Dragon's Gate

1989 *Boston Globe–Horn Book* Nonfiction Honor Book
  The Rainbow People

1977 *Boston Globe–Horn Book* Fiction Award
  Child of the Owl

1976 *Boston Globe–Horn Book* Fiction Honor Book
1976 Carter G. Woodson Book Award
1976 Newbery Honor Book
  Dragonwings

> *"Probably the reason why much of my writing has found its way to a teenage audience is that I'm always pursuing the theme of being an outsider—an alien—and many teenagers feel they're aliens. All of my books have dealt with the outsider."*

Dragonwings, published in 1975, tells the story of a young Chinese man, Moon Shadow, who travels to America to be with his father, Windrider.

Many of the characters in *Dragonwings,* which was named a Newbery Honor book, were included in Dragon's Gate, a story about people struggleing to live within two very different cultures.

In *The Star Fisher,* Yep returns to another place he had heard about over and over as a child. His mother was born in Ohio but spent much of her childhood in Clarksburg, West Virginia. Her father—Laurence's grandfather—had opened a laundry there. The family became the first Asians to live in Clarksburg. Joan Lee, the heroine of *The Star Fisher,* is much like Yep's own mother. She feels the pain of racism but also the joy of seeing and learning new things.

In retelling the stories he heard from his parents and grandparents, Laurence Yep writes history colored by memory. Yep has not, however, forgotten his first love of science fiction and fantasy. His works include *Dragon of the Lost Sea* and *Dragon Cauldren.* He has also retold

YEP TELLS YOUNG WRITERS TO USE ALL OF THEIR SENSES AS PART OF THE 'CREATIVE PROCESS.' HE SAYS TOO MANY WRITERS "JUST USE THEIR EYES."

Chinese legends and folktales. Once a boy who believed he wasn't part of any one culture, Yep has become an expert guide to unknown worlds, both alien and earthbound.

❧

WHERE TO FIND OUT MORE ABOUT LAURENCE YEP

BOOKS

Drew, Bernard A. *The 100 Most Popular Young Adult Authors: Biographical Sketches and Bibliographies.* Englewood, Colo.: Libraries Unlimited, 1997.

Johnson-Feelings, Dianne. *Presenting Laurence Yep.* New York: Twayne Publications, 1995.

Kovacs, Deborah, and James Preller. *Meet the Authors and Illustrators: 60 Creators of Favorite Children's Books Talk about Their Work.* Vol. 2. New York: Scholastic, 1993.

Zia, Helen, and Susan B. Gall, eds. *Notable Asian Americans.* Detroit: Gale Research, 1995.

WEB SITES

EDUCATIONAL PAPERBACK ASSOCIATION
http://www.edupaperback.org/authorbios/Yep_Laurence.html
To read a biography of Laurence Yep

HOUGHTON MIFFLIN READING
http://www.eduplace.com/kids/hmr/mtai/yep.html
To learn more about Laurence Yep

LAURENCE YEP
http://scils.rutgers.edu/~kvander/yep.html
For information about Yep's life and work

———

WHEN YEP WAS SEVENTEEN, A TEACHER TOLD HIS CLASS THAT TO EARN AN A THEY HAD TO GET SOMETHING PUBLISHED IN A NATIONAL MAGAZINE. THE TEACHER LATER CHANGED HIS MIND, BUT BY THEN YEP HAD ALREADY BECOME A WRITER.

Jane Yolen

Born: February 11, 1939

Jane Yolen's great grandfather was a *reb,* a storyteller, in Russia. Even as a small girl, Jane knew she had been blessed with this gift. As soon as she was able to put words down on paper, she knew she would become a writer. Today, after writing nearly 300 books of folklore, fantasy, poetry, science fiction, history, and religion— for both children and adults— new ideas still bubble to the surface faster than she can catch them.

Jane Yolen was born on February 11, 1939, in New York City. Jane's father was a newspaper writer and an international kite-flying

---

YOLEN'S *OWL MOON* RECEIVED THE 1988 CALDECOTT MEDAL FOR ITS ILLUSTRATIONS BY JOHN SCHOENHERR.

champion. Her mother was a social worker and created crossword puzzles for magazines. After attending high school in Connecticut, Yolen went to Smith College in Massachusetts. She returned to New York City following graduation and began working in the publishing industry.

In 1962, Yolen married a computer scientist named David Stemple. A few years later, Yolen and Stemple left

> *"Folklore is the perfect second skin. From under its hide, we can see all the shimmering, shadowy uncertainties of the world."*

their jobs and spent a year traveling through Europe and the Middle East. Everywhere she went, Yolen talked to people and learned about their lives and culture. She has tried to use their tales in her writing ever since.

When Yolen and Stemple returned to the United States, they settled in a rambling farmhouse in western Massachusetts. Yolen soon gave birth to the first of her three children. She also began her full-time career as a writer, musician, storyteller, lecturer, and literary critic.

Yolen chooses her words carefully. She composes her books the way a musician writes a song. The sound of the words—their rhythm and melody—is just as important, she says, as their meaning. In fact, she never considers a piece of writing complete until she has read it out loud.

YOLEN COMPLETED *AN INVITATION TO THE BUTTERFLY BALL: A COUNTING RHYME* IN JUST THREE DAYS, BUT IT TOOK HER NINETEEN YEARS TO WRITE *THE STONE SILENUS*.

A Selected Bibliography of Yolen's Work

Atalanta and the Arcadian Beast (2003)

Firebird (2002)

Girl in a Cage (2002)

Hippolyta and the Curse of the Amazons (2002)

Harvest Home (2000)

Where Have the Unicorns Gone? (2000)

Moon Ball (1999)

Armageddon Summer (1998)

The One-Armed Queen (1998)

Child of Faerie, Child of Earth (1997)

Dragon's Blood (1996)

And Twelve Chinese Acrobats (1994)

Letting Swift River Go (1992)

All Those Secrets of the World (1991)

The Devil's Arithmetic (1988)

Owl Moon (1987)

The Stone Silenus (1984)

Sleeping Ugly (1981)

Commander Toad in Space (1980)

Dream Weaver (1979)

An Invitation to the Butterfly Ball: A Counting Rhyme (1976)

The Girl Who Cried Flowers and Other Tales (1974)

The Girl Who Loved the Wind (1972)

The Emperor and the Kite (1967)

Pirates in Petticoats (1963)

She waits to be struck by a feeling that's something like love. When she feels it, she knows the work is right.

Among her best-loved picture books are *Owl Moon, The Girl Who Loved the Wind,* and *Letting Swift River Go.* The stories in the Pit Dragon trilogy are high fantasy for young adults. And *The Girl Who Cried Flowers and Other Tales* brings together many of Jane Yolen's finest qualities: beautiful language, magic, originality, and a gentle handling of death, kindness, and love.

"Ideas come from all over. It is what one does with the ideas that makes the difference."

As the author of many original folk and fairy tales, Jane Yolen has been called "America's Hans Christian Andersen." As flattering as this may be, Yolen feels it's a bit like being asked to walk in boots that are too big. She is just happy that in her long career she has been able to discover new stories, write them down, and share them with eager readers.

❧

WHERE TO FIND OUT MORE ABOUT JANE YOLEN

BOOKS

Drew, Bernard A. *The 100 Most Popular Young Adult Authors:*
Biographical Sketches and Bibliographies.
Englewood, Colo.: Libraries Unlimited, 1996.

Roginski, James W. *Behind the Covers: Interviews with*
Authors and Illustrators of Books for Children and Young Adults.
Englewood, Colo.: Libraries Unlimited, 1985.

Something about the Author.
Vol. 75. Detroit: Gale Research, 1994.

WEB SITES

JANE YOLEN'S OFFICIAL WEB SITE
http://www.janeyolen.com/
For more information about the Jane Yolen's work

INTERNET PUBLIC LIBRARY
http://www.ipl.org/youth/AskAuthor/Yolen.html
To read a biography of and a short interview with Jane Yolen

———

YOLEN'S TALENT WAS RECOGNIZED EARLY, AT LEAST BY HER CLASSMATES AND TEACHER. TO THEM, SHE BECAME FAMOUS AFTER WRITING THE CLASS MUSICAL ABOUT TALKING VEGETABLES. YOLEN PLAYED THE ROLE OF A CARROT.

Ed Young

Born: November 28, 1931

When Ed Young was a student, his mother was not sure he would ever be successful. He did not get very good grades in school. Instead, he would daydream and think about drawing pictures and becoming an artist. Young went on to become a successful writer and illustrator of children's books. His best-known books include *High on a Hill: A Book of Chinese Riddle, Lon Po Po: A Red-Riding Hood Story from China,* and *Cat and Rat: The Legend of the Chinese Zodiac.* Young has also illustrated many books for other authors.

Ed Young was born on November 28, 1931, in Tientsin, China. When he was about three years old, he and his family moved to Shanghai, a much larger city. European countries controlled the area where Ed lived, so it was difficult for his family to buy the things they needed. But Ed's parents worked hard and

ALONG WITH WORKING AS A CHILDREN'S BOOK ILLUSTRATOR, YOUNG HAS
TAUGHT ART AT SEVERAL ART SCHOOLS AND UNIVERSITIES.

provided a comfortable life for their family.

From an early age, Ed loved to create stories and draw pictures. He often showed his drawings to friends of the family. Many people were impressed with Ed's talent, and they thought he should be an artist. But his father wanted him to study architecture.

Ed Young went to Hong Kong to finish high school.

"A Chinese painting is often accompanied by words. They are complementary. There are things that words do that pictures never can, and likewise, there are images that words can never describe."

A Selected Bibliography of Young's Work

What about Me? (2002)
Monkey King (2001)
The Hunter: A Chinese Folktale (Illustrations only, 2000)
White Wave: A Chinese Tale (Illustrations only, 1996)
Cat and Rat: The Legend of the Chinese Zodiac (1995)
Seven Blind Mice (Illustrations and retelling, 1992)
What Comes in Spring? (Illustrations only, 1992)
While I Sleep (Illustrations only, 1992)
Goodbye, Geese (Illustrations only, 1991)
Lon Po Po: A Red-Riding Hood Story from China (Illustrations and translation, 1989)
In the Night, Still Dark (Illustrations only, 1988)
Foolish Rabbit's Big Mistake (Illustrations only, 1985)
The Double Life of Pocahontas (Illustrations only, 1983)
Yeh-Shen: A Cinderella Story from China (Illustrations only, 1982)
High on a Hill: A Book of Chinese Riddles (1980)
Tales from the Arabian Nights (Illustrations only, 1978)
The Emperor and the Kite (Illustrations only, 1967)
The Mean Mouse and Other Mean Stories (Illustrations only, 1962)

Young's Major Literary Awards

1993 Caldecott Honor Book
1992 *Boston Globe–Horn Book* Picture Book Award
    Seven Blind Mice

1990 *Boston Globe–Horn Book* Picture Book Award
1990 Caldecott Medal
    Lon Po Po: A Red-Riding Hood Story from China

1984 *Boston Globe–Horn Book* Nonfiction Award
    The Double Life of Pocahontas

1983 *Boston Globe–Horn Book* Picture Book Honor Book
    Yeh-Shen: A Cinderella Story from China

1968 Caldecott Honor Book
    The Emperor and the Kite

About two and a half years later, he came to the United States to attend college and study architecture. After about three years, Young realized he had made a mistake. He loved art, and so he decided to attend an art school. He finished art school three years later and moved to New York City to become an illustrator.

Young's first job was with an advertising agency. During his lunch breaks, he sketched animals at a nearby zoo. He ended up with a large collection of illustrations.

"Before I am involved with a project, I must be moved, and as I grow, I try to create something exciting. It is my purpose to stimulate growth in the reader as an active participant."

When the advertising agency went out of business, Young's friends suggested that he become an illustrator for children's books. He showed his drawings to a publisher, and he was hired to illustrate *The Mean Mouse and Other Mean Stories,* written by Janice Udry. The book was published in 1962. Since then, he has done the illustrations for many other books by Jane Yolen, Jean Fritz, and Al-Ling Louie among others.

In addition to illustrating books, Young has written his own children's books, some of which are retellings of folktales or fables. Many Chinese folktales and stories that he has retold are ones he remembers

YOUNG OFTEN TRAVELS TO DO RESEARCH ON ANIMALS HE IS ILLUSTRATING. HE BELIEVES THAT IT IS IMPORTANT TO SEE THE ANIMALS IN THEIR OWN ENVIRONMENT, TO WATCH THEM MOVE, AND TO HEAR THE SOUNDS THEY MAKE.

hearing as a child. Young does a lot of research on these folktales to make sure they are accurate.

Young lives with his family in Hastings-on-Hudson, New York. He visits China frequently to see relatives who still live there, and he continues to write and illustrate children's books.

&

WHERE TO FIND OUT MORE ABOUT ED YOUNG

BOOKS

Marantz, Sylvia S. *Artists of the Page: Interviews with Children's Book Illustrators.*
Jefferson, N.C.: McFarland, 1992.

Silvey, Anita, ed. *Children's Books and Their Creators.*
Boston: Houghton Mifflin, 1995.

Something about the Author. Vol. 74. Detroit: Gale Research, 1993.

WEB SITES

ED YOUNG BIOGRAPHY
http://www2.scholastic.com/teachers/authorsandbooks/authorstudies/
authorhome.jhtml?authorID=216&collateralID=5311&displayName=Biography
To learn more about author and illustrator Ed Young

EDUCATIONAL PAPERBACK ASSOCIATION
http://www.edupaperback.org/authorbios/Young_Ed.html
For information about Young's life

IN SCHOOL, ED YOUNG DIDN'T ALWAYS BRING HOME GOOD GRADES. HE STILL REMEMBERS HIS MOTHER WORRYING ABOUT WHAT HE WOULD DO WITH HIS LIFE.

Paul O. Zelinsky

Born: February 14, 1953

Paul O. Zelinsky published his first piece of artwork in *Highlights* magazine in 1957—when he was still in nursery school! It was just the first of many honors this amazingly talented artist has earned during his career as a book illustrator.

Paul O. Zelinsky was born in Evanston, Illinois, on February 14, 1953. His father taught college mathematics, his mother illustrated medical books, and young Paul drew. Because his father taught at several different colleges, the family moved around during Paul's childhood. Though Paul frequently had to change schools and get used to new towns, his love of drawing always stayed the same.

WHEN ZELINSKY ILLUSTRATED *THE STORY OF MRS. LOVEWRIGHT AND PURRLESS HER CAT*, HE SAW THE BOOK AS HAVING "A TANGY QUALITY." HE CAPTURED THAT TANGINESS BY THINKING OF A DILL PICKLE.

Although he loved art, Paul never thought about becoming an illustrator when he grew up. Instead, he imagined himself as a ventriloquist, an architect, or perhaps a teacher of natural history. It wasn't until Zelinsky went to Yale University and took a course taught by Maurice Sendak, the writer and illustrator of *Where the Wild Things Are,* that he realized he might enjoy a career illustrating children's books.

It didn't happen right away. Zelinsky did a few illustrations for the *New York Times,* went on to get a master's degree in painting, and tried teaching. He admits, "I was a lousy teacher." Finally, in 1978, he illustrated his first children's book, Avi's *Emily Upham's Revenge: A Massachusetts Adventure.* Three years later, Zelinsky wrote and illustrated his own book, *The Maid and the Mouse and the Odd-Shape House: A Story in Rhyme.*

> *"I try to make the book talk, as it talks to me, and not worry whether it is in my style or not. . . . I get a kick out of doing each book differently."*

Since then, Zelinsky has written or illustrated several additional books for young readers. His work is known for its richness, humor, and variety. No two books are ever alike. As he himself says, "I've recently decided that I should be recognized by my unrecognizability."

The children who pore over his books and the adults who hand out

WHEN ZELINSKY WAS WORKING ON BEVERLY CLEARY'S *RALPH S. MOUSE,* HE VISITED A CLASSROOM TO SEE HOW REAL FIFTH GRADERS LOOKED AND ACTED. AND HE BOUGHT TWO MICE TO SEE HOW REAL MICE LOOKED AND ACTED.

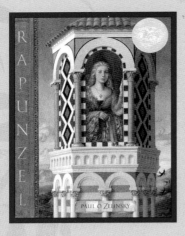

A Selected Bibliography of Zelinsky's Work

Wet Magic (2001)

Awful Ogre's Awful Day (Illustrations only, 2000)

The Magic City (Illustrations only, 2000)

Five Children and It (Illustrations only, 1999)

Rapunzel (Illustrations only, 1997)

Swamp Angel (Illustrations only, 1994)

The Enchanted Castle (Illustrations only, 1992)

The Wheels on the Bus (Illustrations only, 1990)

Rumpelstiltskin (Illustrations only, 1986)

The Story of Mrs. Lovewright and Purrless Her Cat
(Illustrations only, 1985)

Hansel and Gretel (Illustrations only, 1984)

Dear Mr. Henshaw (Illustrations only, 1983)

Ralph S. Mouse (Illustrations only, 1982)

*The Maid and the Mouse and the Odd-Shape
House: A Story in Rhyme* (1981)

How I Hunted the Little Fellows (Illustrations only, 1979)

Emily Upham's Revenge: A Massachusetts Adventure
(Illustrations only, 1978)

Zelinsky's Major Literary Awards

1998 Caldecott Medal
   Rapunzel

1995 *Boston Globe–Horn Book* Picture Book Honor Book
1995 Caldecott Honor Book
   Swamp Angel

1987 Caldecott Honor Book
   Rumpelstiltskin

1985 Caldecott Honor Book
   Hansel and Gretel

awards don't seem to mind this "unrecognizability." Zelinsky has illustrated classic fairy tales such as *Rumpelstiltskin* and *Rapunzel*, tall tales such as *Swamp Angel*, realistic books such as *Dear Mr. Henshaw*, fantasies such as *The Magic City*, picture books such as the gruesomely funny *Awful Ogre's Awful Day*, and the famous pop-up entitled *The Wheels on the Bus*. The list goes on and on. Sometimes Zelinsky's artwork looks as if it belongs in an art museum. Sometimes it looks like rustic folk art. And sometimes it's as bright and funny and modern as a ten-year-old kid's art.

Paul O. Zelinsky has won just about every award given for children's book illustration.

Hansel and Gretel, Rumpelstiltskin, and *Swamp Angel* were all named Caldecott Honor Books, and in 1998, *Rapunzel* was awarded the Caldecott Medal.

Paul O. Zelinsky lives in Brooklyn, New York, with his wife, Deborah. He has two daughters—Anna and Rachel—and many more creative ideas waiting to come to life.

> "It's a great deal of fun, this work. I learn things. I make things. And I feel I get to change my mind all the time about what I want to do."

WHERE TO FIND OUT MORE ABOUT PAUL O. ZELINSKY

BOOKS

Cummings, Pat. *Talking With Artists, Vol. 3: Conversations with Peter Catalanotto, Raul Colon, Lisa Desimini, Jane Dyer, Kevin Hawkes, G. Brian Karas, Betsy Lewin, Ted Lewin, Keiko Narahashi, Elise Primavera, Anna Rich, Peter Sís and Paul O. Zelinsky.* Boston: Houghton Mifflin, 1999.

Holtze, Sally Holmes, ed. *Sixth Book of Junior Authors & Illustrators.* New York: H. W. Wilson Company, 1989.

WEB SITES

AUTOBIOGRAPHY FROM CHILDREN'S BOOK COUNCIL
http://www.cbcbooks.org/html/pozelinsky.html
To read what Zelinsky says about his version of *Rumpelstiltskin*

THE SCOOP: PAUL O. ZELINSKY
http://www.friend.ly.net/scoop/biographies/zelinskypaul/
For information about Paul O. Zelinsky's life and a sample of his illustrations

IN THEIR YOUTH, ZELINSKY AND HIS FRIEND TRIED TO PUBLISH A BOOK ABOUT AN ALIEN APE WHO SAVES THE WORLD FROM EVIL GORILLAS. NO ONE WAS INTERESTED IN PUBLISHING THE FANTASTIC TALE.

Paul Zindel

Born: May 15, 1936

Writing stories about teenagers comes naturally to Paul Zindel. Few people can match his ability to write from a teen's point of view with honesty and humor. His novels have helped to create a special category of literature—young adult fiction. In addition to his books for young adults, Paul Zindel has also written several renowned plays. All of Zindel's novels begin with real, specific moments from his

own life. He makes his characters believable by putting a piece of himself into each of them. In his work, readers meet some of the people and touch on events from his own troubled childhood. They also learn the lessons that he has learned.

Paul Zindel was born on May 15, 1936, on Staten Island, New York. His father deserted the family when Paul was only two. His mother often moved with Paul and his sister, looking for work.

ZINDEL ENJOYS READING WORKS BY OTHER YOUNG ADULT WRITERS; INCLUDING PAULA DANZIGER, PATRICIA MACLACHLAN, AND LIZ LEVY.

As a result, Paul never had close friends and spent much of his time alone. But he had an active imagination and found ways to entertain himself with puppets, comic books, and movies.

In high school, Paul began writing plays. His interest in theater continued to grow in college. At Wagner College on Staten Island, Zindel took a course taught by playwright Edward Albee, who had a great influence on his writing.

After graduating with a chemistry degree, Zindel began teaching chemistry and physics at Tottenville High School on Staten Island.

In his spare time, Zindel continued to write plays, including *The Effect of Gamma Rays on*

A Selected Bibliography of Zindel's Work

The Gadget (2001)
Night of the Bat (2001)
Rats (1999)
Reef of Death (1998)
The Doom Stone (1995)
David & Della (1993)
Fifth Grade Safari (1993)
The Pigman & Me (1991)
A Begonia for Miss Applebaum (1989)
The Amazing and Death-Defying Diary of Eugene Dingman (1987)
Harry and Hortense at Hormone High (1984)
The Girl Who Wanted a Boy (1981)
The Pigman's Legacy (1980)
The Undertaker's Gone Bananas (1978)
Confessions of a Teenage Baboon (1977)
Pardon Me, You're Stepping on My Eyeball! (1976)
I Love My Mother (1975)
Let Me Hear You Whisper (1974)
The Secret Affairs of Margaret Wild (1973)
The Effect of Gamma Rays on Man-in-the-Moon Marigolds (1971)
I Never Loved Your Mind (1970)
My Darling, My Hamburger (1969)
The Pigman (1968)

Zindel's Major Literary Awards

1969 *Boston Globe–Horn Book* Fiction Honor Book
   The Pigman

Man-in-the-Moon Marigolds in 1963. The play opened on Broadway in 1971 and won many awards, including an Obie Award, a New York Drama Critics' Circle Award, and the Pulitzer Prize.

> *"I like storytelling. We all have an active thing that we do that gives us self-esteem, that makes us proud; it's necessary. I have to tell stories because that's the way the wiring went in."*

Zindel's first and best-known novel is *The Pigman,* published in 1968. It is based on a common Zindel theme: troubled teenagers befriending adults. Through tragedy, the teens learn about themselves and how to cope with life and death.

A year after Zindel published his first novel, he quit teaching. He believed that he could do more for teenagers as a writer than as a teacher. In 1973, he married Bonnie Hildebrand. They have two children, David Jack and Elizabeth Claire.

Writing keeps Paul Zindel very busy. In addition to his many young adult novels, he has written a children's book, a series of books for middle-grade readers (the Wacky Facts Lunch Bunch series),

> *"I like to write for kids about worlds they can identify with—worlds they know that they're interested in and worlds that have characters who are solving problems that they themselves would want to solve."*

and several plays and movie screenplays. His work brings humor and

----

ZINDEL HAS WORKED AS A WAITER, A BARTENDER, A DANCE INSTRUCTOR, A CHEMIST, A CHIMNEY SWEEP, AND A TECHNICAL WRITER.

hope to people struggling to make sense of life. He offers teens a different view of the world and gives them meaning as they journey through it. Zindel's message is clear: "It is glorious to be young and to be involved in the great adventure of life."

❧

WHERE TO FIND OUT MORE ABOUT PAUL ZINDEL

BOOKS

Drew, Bernard A. *The 100 Most Popular Young Adult Authors: Biographical Sketches and Bibliographies.* Englewood, Colo.: Libraries Unlimited, 1997.

Hedblad, Alan, ed. *Something about the Author.* Vol. 102. Detroit: Gale Research, 1999.

Zindel, Paul. *The Pigman and Me.* New York: HarperCollins, 1992.

WEB SITES

AUTHORS ONLINE TRANSCRIPT
http://www2.scholastic.com/teachers/authorsandbooks/authorstudies/ authorhome.jhtml?authorID=217&collateralID=5312&displayName=Biography
For information about Zindel and his work

AUTHORS/ILLUSTRATORS
http://www.randomhouse.com/teachers/authors/zind.html
For an interview with, fun facts about, and comments by Paul Zindel

---

ZINDEL KEEPS A JOURNAL THAT HE USES FOR INSPIRATION. IN IT HE PUTS NOTES, TAPE RECORDINGS, PHOTOS, VIDEO EXCERPTS, MOVIE STILLS, POEMS, MAGAZINE CLIPPINGS, AND NEWSPAPER ARTICLES.

Gene Zion

Born: October 5, 1913
Died: December 5, 1975

Gene Zion had what one critic called a gift for seeing a story "through the eyes of the child." His books have charmed readers for decades and will entertain young people for many years to come.

Gene Zion was born in New York City on October 5, 1913. He grew up in nearby Ridgefield, New Jersey. "Life was rural," he wrote later, "and included a barn with a cow, chickens, and pigeons." Gene started drawing in kindergarten and decided early on that he wanted to do something creative with his life.

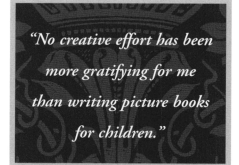

"No creative effort has been more gratifying for me than writing picture books for children."

Zion attended the New School for Social Research and the Pratt Institute in New York City. He studied advertising art, and in 1936 he designed a travel poster that won a contest. As a result, he got

ZION'S ORIGINAL TYPEWRITTEN MANUSCRIPTS OF HIS BOOKS STILL EXIST. THEY ARE IN THE LIBRARY AT THE UNIVERSITY OF MINNESOTA.

to travel and live in Europe for a while. There he visited printing plants and became interested in making books.

When World War II (1939–1945) began, Zion joined the army. His job was to design training manuals and filmstrips to teach soldiers in the antiaircraft artillery. After the war, he worked for the CBS radio network and for several magazine publishers. Eventually, he became a freelance designer.

By this time, Zion had married artist and illustrator Margaret Bloy Graham. Graham and the great children's book editor Ursula Nordstrom persuaded Zion to try writing a picture book. Zion looked at a sketch his wife had made years

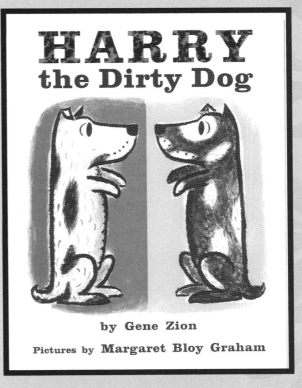

A Selected Bibliography of Zion's Work

Harry by the Sea (1965)
The Sugar Mouse Cake (1964)
The Meanest Squirrel I Ever Met (1962)
Harry and the Lady Next Door (1960)
The Plant Sitter (1959)
No Roses for Harry (1958)
Dear Garbage Man (1957)
Jeffie's Party (1957)
Harry the Dirty Dog (1956)
Really Spring (1956)
Summer Snowman (1955)
Hide and Seek Day (1954)
All Falling Down (1951)

before of children gathering apples in an orchard. It gave him the idea for *All Falling Down*, his first book.

The story, like all of Zion's stories, is very simple. It is hardly more than a list of things that fall down, such as apples, leaves, and snow. The book, which included illustrations by Graham, was very successful, however.

Zion and Graham worked together on thirteen books. Their best-known books are about Harry the Dog. The first was *Harry the Dirty Dog*, in which Harry, a white dog with black spots, gets so dirty that he becomes a black dog with white spots. His owners don't even recognize him until Harry breaks down and takes a bath. Harry is portrayed in few words and through simple pictures, but he is a memorable character, and his books have been popular ever since.

> *"Harry was a white dog with black spots who liked everything, except . . . getting a bath."*
> —Harry the Dirty Dog

Zion and Graham wrote four Harry the Dog books. The last was *Harry by the Sea,* published in 1965, in which Harry gets lost at the beach. When he returns, he's a mess again and looks like a creature made of seaweed.

HARRY THE DIRTY DOG HAS BEEN ADAPTED FOR A NUMBER OF CHILDREN'S THEATER PRODUCTIONS.

Zion and Margaret Bloy Graham divorced in 1968. Zion died on December 5, 1975. Almost five decades after its publication, his *Harry the Dirty Dog* is still in print.

❧

WHERE TO FIND OUT MORE ABOUT GENE ZION

BOOKS

Fuller, Muriel, ed. *More Junior Authors.*
New York: H. W. Wilson Company, 1963.

WEB SITES

HALL KIDS TALES
http://hallkidstales.com/Z/8.shtml
For a review and a synopsis of each of Gene Zion's children's books

UNIVERSITY OF MINNESOTA LIBRARIES
http://special.lib.umn.edu/findaid/html/clrc/clrc0201.html
To read a short biography of Zion

ZION FIRST WORKED AS A PROFESSIONAL ARTIST WHEN HE WAS A SCHOOLBOY. HIS FRIENDS USED TO PAY HIM TO PAINT PICTURES ON THE BACK OF THEIR YELLOW RAIN SLICKERS.

INDEX